Connected Mathematics 2

Implementing and Teaching Guide

Glenda Lappan

James T. Fey

William M. Fitzgerald

Susan Friel

Elizabeth Difanis Phillips

PEARSON

Prentice Hall

Boston, Massachusetts
Upper Saddle River, New Jersey

Connected Mathematics™ Project was developed at Michigan State University with financial support from the Michigan State University Office of the Provost, Computing and Technology, and the College of Natural Science.

Connected Mathematics™ is based upon work supported by the National Science Foundation under Grant No. MDR 9150217 and Grant No. ESI 9986372. Opinions expressed are those of the authors and not necessarily those of the Foundation.

The Michigan State University authors and administration have agreed that all MSU royalties arising from this publication will be devoted to purposes supported by the Department of Mathematics and the MSU Mathematics Enrichment Fund.

Acknowledgments The people who made up the *Connected Mathematics 2* team—representing editorial, editorial services, design services, and production services—are listed below. Bold type denotes core team members.

Leora Adler, Judith Buice, Kerry Cashman, Patrick Culleton, Sheila DeFazio, Katie Hallahan, Richard Heater, **Barbara Holllingdale, Jayne Holman,** Karen Holtzman, **Etta Jacobs,** Christine Lee, Carolyn Lock, Catherine Maglio, **Dotti Marshall,** Rich McMahon, Eve Melnechuk, Terri Mitchell, **Marsha Novak,** Irene Rubin, Donna Russo, Robin Samper, Siri Schwartzman, **Nancy Smith,** Emily Soltanoff, **Mark Tricca,** Paula Vergith, Roberta Warshaw, Helen Young.

ISBN 0-13-133947-8

4 5 6 7 8 9 10   09 08 07 06

Authors of Connected Mathematics

(from left to right) Glenda Lappan, Betty Phillips, Susan Friel, Bill Fitzgerald, Jim Fey

Glenda Lappan is a University Distinguished Professor in the Department of Mathematics at Michigan State University. Her research and development interests are in the connected areas of students' learning of mathematics and mathematics teachers' professional growth and change related to the development and enactment of K–12 curriculum materials.

James T. Fey is a Professor of Curriculum and Instruction and Mathematics at the University of Maryland. His consistent professional interest has been development and research focused on curriculum materials that engage middle and high school students in problem-based collaborative investigations of mathematical ideas and their applications.

William M. Fitzgerald (*Deceased*) was a Professor in the Department of Mathematics at Michigan State University. His early research was on the use of concrete materials in supporting student learning and led to the development of teaching materials for laboratory environments. Later he helped develop a teaching model to support student experimentation with mathematics.

Susan N. Friel is a Professor of Mathematics Education in the School of Education at the University of North Carolina at Chapel Hill. Her research interests focus on statistics education for middle-grade students and, more broadly, on teachers' professional development and growth in teaching mathematics K–8.

Elizabeth Difanis Phillips is a Senior Academic Specialist in the Mathematics Department of Michigan State University. She is interested in teaching and learning mathematics for both teachers and students. These interests have led to curriculum and professional development projects at the middle school and high school levels, as well as projects related to the teaching and learning of algebra across the grades.

CMP2 Development Staff

Advisory Board for CMP2

Field Test Sites for CMP2

During the development of the revised edition of *Connected Mathematics* (CMP2), more than 100 classroom teachers have field-tested materials at 49 school sites in 12 states and the District of Columbia. This classroom testing occurred over three academic years (2001 through 2004), allowing careful study of the effectiveness of each of the 24 units that comprise the program. A special thanks to the students and teachers at these pilot schools.

Arkansas
Magnolia Public Schools
Kittena Bell*, Judith Trowell*; *Central Elementary School:* Maxine Broom, Betty Eddy, Tiffany Fallin, Bonnie Flurry, Carolyn Monk, Elizabeth Tye; *Magnolia Junior High School:* Monique Bryan, Ginger Cook, David Graham, Shelby Lamkin

Colorado
Boulder Public Schools
Nevin Platt Middle School: Judith Koenig
St. Vrain Valley School District, Longmont
Westview Middle School: Colleen Beyer, Kitty Canupp, Ellie Decker*, Peggy McCarthy, Tanya deNobrega, Cindy Payne, Ericka Pilon, Andrew Roberts

District of Columbia
Capitol Hill Day School: Ann Lawrence

Georgia
University of Georgia, Athens
Brad Findell
Madison Public Schools
Morgan County Middle School: Renee Burgdorf, Lynn Harris, Nancy Kurtz, Carolyn Stewart

Maine
Falmouth Public Schools
Falmouth Middle School: Donna Erikson, Joyce Hebert, Paula Hodgkins, Rick Hogan, David Legere, Cynthia Martin, Barbara Stiles, Shawn Towle*

Michigan
Portland Public Schools
Portland Middle School: Mark Braun, Holly DeRosia, Kathy Dole*, Angie Foote, Teri Keusch, Tammi Wardwell
Traverse City Area Public Schools
Bertha Vos Elementary: Kristin Sak; *Central Grade School:* Michelle Clark; Jody Meyers; *Eastern Elementary:* Karrie Tufts; *Interlochen Elementary:* Mary McGee-Cullen; *Long Lake Elementary:* Julie Faulkner*, Charlie Maxbauer, Katherine Sleder; *Norris Elementary:* Hope Slanaker; *Oak Park Elementary:* Jessica Steed; *Traverse Heights Elementary:* Jennifer Wolfert; *Westwoods Elementary:* Nancy Conn; *Old Mission Peninsula School:* Deb Larimer; *Traverse City East Junior High:* Ivanka Berkshire, Ruthanne Kladder, Jan Palkowski, Jane Peterson, Mary Beth Schmitt; *Traverse City West Junior High:* Dan Fouch*, Ray Fouch
Sturgis Public Schools
Sturgis Middle School: Ellen Eisele

Minnesota
Burnsville School District 191
Hidden Valley Elementary: Stephanie Cin, Jane McDevitt
Hopkins School District 270
Alice Smith Elementary: Sandra Cowing, Kathleen Gustafson, Martha Mason, Scott Stillman; *Eisenhower Elementary:* Chad Bellig, Patrick Berger, Nancy Glades, Kye Johnson, Shane Wasserman, Victoria Wilson; *Gatewood Elementary:* Sarah Ham, Julie Kloos, Janine Pung, Larry Wade; *Glen Lake Elementary:* Jacqueline Cramer, Kathy Hering, Cecelia Morris, Robb Trenda; *Katherine Curren Elementary:* Diane Bancroft, Sue DeWit, John Wilson; *L. H. Tanglen Elementary:* Kevin Athmann, Lisa Becker, Mary LaBelle, Kathy Rezac, Roberta Severson; *Meadowbrook Elementary:* Jan Gauger, Hildy Shank, Jessica Zimmerman; *North Junior High:* Laurel Hahn, Kristin Lee, Jodi Markuson, Bruce Mestemacher, Laurel Miller, Bonnie Rinker, Jeannine Salzer, Sarah Shafer, Cam Stottler; *West Junior High:* Alicia Beebe, Kristie Earl, Nobu Fujii, Pam Georgetti, Susan Gilbert, Regina Nelson Johnson, Debra Lindstrom, Michele Luke*, Jon Sorensen
Minneapolis School District 1
Ann Sullivan K–8 School: Bronwyn Collins; Anne Bartel* (Curriculum and Instruction Office)
Wayzata School District 284
Central Middle School: Sarajane Myers, Dan Nielsen, Tanya Ravnholdt
White Bear Lake School District 624
Central Middle School: Amy Jorgenson, Michelle Reich, Brenda Sammon

New York
New York City Public Schools
IS 89: Yelena Aynbinder, Chi-Man Ng, Nina Rapaport, Joel Spengler, Phyllis Tam*, Brent Wyso; *Wagner Middle School:* Jason Appel, Intissar Fernandez, Yee Gee Get, Richard Goldstein, Irving Marcus, Sue Norton, Bernadita Owens, Jennifer Rehn*, Kevin Yuhas

* indicates a Field Test Site Coordinator

Ohio

Talawanda School District, Oxford
Talawanda Middle School: Teresa Abrams, Larry Brock, Heather Brosey, Julie Churchman, Monna Even, Karen Fitch, Bob George, Amanda Klee, Pat Meade, Sandy Montgomery, Barbara Sherman, Lauren Steidl

Miami University
Jeffrey Wanko*

Springfield Public Schools
Rockway School: Jim Mamer

Pennsylvania

Pittsburgh Public Schools
Kenneth Labuskes, Marianne O'Connor, Mary Lynn Raith*; *Arthur J. Rooney Middle School:* David Hairston, Stamatina Mousetis, Alfredo Zangaro; *Frick International Studies Academy:* Suzanne Berry, Janet Falkowski, Constance Finseth, Romika Hodge, Frank Machi; *Reizenstein Middle School:* Jeff Baldwin, James Brautigam, Lorena Burnett, Glen Cobbett, Michael Jordan, Margaret Lazur, Tamar McPherson, Melissa Munnell, Holly Neely, Ingrid Reed, Dennis Reft

Texas

Austin Independent School District
Bedichek Middle School: Lisa Brown, Jennifer Glasscock, Vicki Massey

El Paso Independent School District
Cordova Middle School: Armando Aguirre, Anneliesa Durkes, Sylvia Guzman, Pat Holguin*, William Holguin, Nancy Nava, Laura Orozco, Michelle Peña, Roberta Rosen, Patsy Smith, Jeremy Wolf

Plano Independent School District
Patt Henry, James Wohlgehagen*; *Frankford Middle School:* Mandy Baker, Cheryl Butsch, Amy Dudley, Betsy Eshelman, Janet Greene, Cort Haynes, Kathy Letchworth, Kay Marshall, Kelly McCants, Amy Reck, Judy Scott, Syndy Snyder, Lisa Wang; *Wilson Middle School:* Darcie Bane, Amanda Bedenko, Whitney Evans, Tonelli Hatley, Sarah (Becky) Higgs, Kelly Johnston, Rebecca McElligott, Kay Neuse, Cheri Slocum, Kelli Straight

Washington

Evergreen School District
Shahala Middle School: Nicole Abrahamsen, Terry Coon*, Carey Doyle, Sheryl Drechsler, George Gemma, Gina Helland, Amy Hilario, Darla Lidyard, Sean McCarthy, Tilly Meyer, Willow Nuewelt, Todd Parsons, Brian Pederson, Stan Posey, Shawn Scott, Craig Sjoberg, Lynette Sundstrom, Charles Switzer, Luke Youngblood

Wisconsin

Beaver Dam Unified School District
Beaver Dam Middle School: Jim Braemer, Jeanne Frick, Jessica Greatens, Barbara Link, Dennis McCormick, Karen Michels, Nancy Nichols*, Nancy Palm, Shelly Stelsel, Susan Wiggins

* indicates a Field Test Site Coordinator

Reviews of CMP to Guide Development of CMP2

Before writing for CMP2 began or field tests were conducted, the first edition of *Connected Mathematics* was submitted to the mathematics faculties of school districts from many parts of the country and to 80 individual reviewers for extensive comments.

School District Survey Reviews of CMP

Arizona
Madison School District #38 (Phoenix)

Arkansas
Cabot School District, Little Rock School District, Magnolia School District

California
Los Angeles Unified School District

Colorado
St. Vrain Valley School District (Longmont)

Florida
Leon County Schools (Tallahassee)

Illinois
School District #21 (Wheeling)

Indiana
Joseph L. Block Junior High (East Chicago)

Kentucky
Fayette County Public Schools (Lexington)

Maine
Selection of Schools

Massachusetts
Selection of Schools

Michigan
Sparta Area Schools

Minnesota
Hopkins School District

Texas
Austin Independent School District, The El Paso Collaborative for Academic Excellence, Plano Independent School District

Wisconsin
Platteville Middle School

Individual Reviewers of CMP

Arkansas
Deborah Cramer; Robby Frizzell *(Taylor)*; Lowell Lynde *(University of Arkansas, Monticello)*; Leigh Manzer *(Norfork)*; Lynne Roberts *(Emerson High School, Emerson)*; Tony Timms *(Cabot Public Schools)*; Judith Trowell *(Arkansas Department of Higher Education)*

California
José Alcantar *(Gilroy)*; Eugenie Belcher *(Gilroy)*; Marian Pasternack *(Lowman M. S. T. Center, North Hollywood)*; Susana Pezoa *(San Jose)*; Todd Rabusin *(Hollister)*; Margaret Siegfried *(Ocala Middle School, San Jose)*; Polly Underwood *(Ocala Middle School, San Jose)*

Colorado
Janeane Golliher *(St. Vrain Valley School District, Longmont)*; Judith Koenig *(Nevin Platt Middle School, Boulder)*

Florida
Paige Loggins *(Swift Creek Middle School, Tallahassee)*

Illinois
Jan Robinson *(School District #21, Wheeling)*

Indiana
Frances Jackson *(Joseph L. Block Junior High, East Chicago)*

Kentucky
Natalee Feese *(Fayette County Public Schools, Lexington)*

Maine
Betsy Berry *(Maine Math & Science Alliance, Augusta)*

Maryland
Joseph Gagnon *(University of Maryland, College Park)*; Paula Maccini *(University of Maryland, College Park)*

Massachusetts
George Cobb *(Mt. Holyoke College, South Hadley)*; Cliff Kanold *(University of Massachusetts, Amherst)*

Michigan
Mary Bouck *(Farwell Area Schools)*; Carol Dorer *(Slauson Middle School, Ann Arbor)*; Carrie Heaney *(Forsythe Middle School, Ann Arbor)*; Ellen Hopkins *(Clague Middle School, Ann Arbor)*; Teri Keusch *(Portland Middle School, Portland)*; Valerie Mills *(Oakland Schools, Waterford)*; Mary Beth Schmitt *(Traverse City East Junior High, Traverse City)*; Jack Smith *(Michigan State University, East Lansing)*; Rebecca Spencer *(Sparta Middle School, Sparta)*; Ann Marie Nicoll Turner *(Tappan Middle School, Ann Arbor)*; Scott Turner *(Scarlett Middle School, Ann Arbor)*

Minnesota
Margarita Alvarez *(Olson Middle School, Minneapolis)*; Jane Amundson *(Nicollet Junior High, Burnsville)*; Anne Bartel *(Minneapolis Public Schools)*; Gwen Ranzau Campbell *(Sunrise Park Middle School, White Bear Lake)*; Stephanie Cin *(Hidden Valley Elementary, Burnsville)*; Joan Garfield *(University of Minnesota, Minneapolis)*; Gretchen Hall *(Richfield Middle School, Richfield)*; Jennifer Larson *(Olson Middle School, Minneapolis)*; Michele Luke *(West Junior High, Minnetonka)*; Jeni Meyer *(Richfield Junior High, Richfield)*; Judy Pfingsten *(Inver Grove Heights Middle School, Inver Grove Heights)*; Sarah Shafer *(North Junior High, Minnetonka)*; Genni Steele *(Central Middle School, White Bear Lake)*; Victoria Wilson *(Eisenhower Elementary, Hopkins)*; Paul Zorn *(St. Olaf College, Northfield)*

New York
Debra Altenau-Bartolino *(Greenwich Village Middle School, New York)*; Doug Clements *(University of Buffalo)*; Francis Curcio *(New York University, New York)*; Christine Dorosh *(Clinton School for Writers, Brooklyn)*; Jennifer Rehn *(East Side Middle School, New York)*; Phyllis Tam *(IS 89 Lab School, New York)*;

Marie Turini *(Louis Armstrong Middle School, New York)*; Lucy West *(Community School District 2, New York)*; Monica Witt *(Simon Baruch Intermediate School 104, New York)*

Pennsylvania
Robert Aglietti *(Pittsburgh)*; Sharon Mihalich *(Freeport)*; Jennifer Plumb *(South Hills Middle School, Pittsburgh)*; Mary Lynn Raith *(Pittsburgh Public Schools)*

Texas
Michelle Bittick *(Austin Independent School District)*; Margaret Cregg *(Plano Independent School District)*; Sheila Cunningham *(Klein Independent School District)*; Judy Hill *(Austin Independent School District)*; Patricia Holguin *(El Paso Independent School District)*; Bonnie McNemar *(Arlington)*; Kay Neuse *(Plano Independent School District)*; Joyce Polanco *(Austin Independent School District)*; Marge Ramirez *(University of Texas at El Paso)*; Pat Rossman *(Baker Campus, Austin)*; Cindy Schimek *(Houston)*; Cynthia Schneider *(Charles A. Dana Center, University of Texas at Austin)*; Uri Treisman *(Charles A. Dana Center, University of Texas at Austin)*; Jacqueline Weilmuenster *(Grapevine-Colleyville Independent School District)*; LuAnn Weynand *(San Antonio)*; Carmen Whitman *(Austin Independent School District)*; James Wohlgehagen *(Plano Independent School District)*

Washington
Ramesh Gangolli *(University of Washington, Seattle)*

Wisconsin
Susan Lamon *(Marquette University, Hales Corner)*; Steve Reinhart *(retired, Chippewa Falls Middle School, Eau Claire)*

Table of Contents

Overview

The *Connected Mathematics Project* (CMP) was funded by the National Science Foundation between 1991 and 1997 to develop a mathematics curriculum for grades 6, 7, and 8. The result was *Connected Mathematics,* a complete mathematics curriculum that helps students develop understanding of important concepts, skills, procedures, and ways of thinking and reasoning in number, geometry, measurement, algebra, probability, and statistics.

In 2000, the National Science Foundation funded a revision of the *Connected Mathematics* materials, CMP2, to take advantage of what we learned in the six years that the first edition of CMP has been used in schools. This Implementation Guide elaborates the goals of CMP2, the process we used for the revision, the scope of the curriculum, and a process for implementation that will support student and teacher learning.

CMP: A Curriculum for Students and Teachers

The CMP materials reflect the understanding that teaching and learning are not distinct—"what to teach" and "how to teach it" are inextricably linked. The circumstances in which students learn affect what is learned. The needs of both students and teachers are considered in the development of the CMP curriculum materials. This curriculum helps teachers and those who work to support teachers examine their expectations for students and analyze the extent to which classroom mathematics tasks and teaching practices align with their goals and expectations.

Overarching Goal of CMP

The overarching goal of *Connected Mathematics* is to help students and teachers develop mathematical knowledge, understanding, and skill along with an awareness of and appreciation for the rich connections among mathematical strands and between mathematics and other disciplines. All the CMP curriculum development has been guided by a single mathematical standard.

All students should be able to reason and communicate proficiently in mathematics. They should have knowledge of and skill in the use of the vocabulary, forms of representation, materials, tools, techniques, and intellectual methods of the discipline of mathematics, including the ability to define and solve problems with reason, insight, inventiveness, and technical proficiency.

CMP2 at a Glance

Below are some key features of *Connected Mathematics 2:*

Problem Centered

Important mathematical concepts are embedded in engaging problems. Students develop understanding and skill as they explore the problems, individually, in a group, or with the class.

Practice With Concepts and Related Skills

The in-class development problems and the homework exercises give students practice distributed over time with important concepts, related skills, and algorithms.

Complete Curriculum

The twenty-four *Connected Mathematics 2* units— eight units for each grade—form a complete middle school curriculum that develops mathematical skills and conceptual understanding across mathematical strands. (Three units from the first edition of CMP—*Ruins of Montarek, Data Around Us,* and *Clever Counting*—will continue to be available to help schools reach individual state mathematics expectations.) In addition, the program provides a complete assessment package, including quizzes, tests, and projects.

For Teachers as well as Students

The *Connected Mathematics* materials were written to support teacher learning of both unfamiliar content and pedagogical strategies. The Teacher's Guides include extensive help with mathematics, pedagogy, and assessment.

Research Based

Each *Connected Mathematics* unit was field tested, evaluated, and revised over a five-year period. Approximately 200 teachers and 45,000 students in diverse school settings across the United States participated in the development of the curriculum.

It Works

It works. Research results consistently show CMP students outperform non-CMP students on tests of problem-solving ability, conceptual understanding, and proportional reasoning. And CMP students do as well as, or better than, non-CMP students on tests of basic skills.

Influence of Theory and Research on CMP2 Curriculum

The curriculum, teacher support, and assessment materials that comprise the *Connected Mathematics* program reflect influence from a variety of sources:

- knowledge of theory and research;

- authors' imagination and personal teaching and learning experiences;

- advice from teachers, mathematicians, teacher educators, curriculum developers, and mathematics education researchers;

- advice from teachers and students who used pilot and field-test versions of the materials.

The fundamental features of the CMP program—focus on big ideas of middle grades mathematics, teaching through student-centered exploration of mathematically rich problems, and continual assessment to inform instruction—reflect the distillation of advice and experience from those varied sources.

Our work was influenced in significant ways by what we knew of existing theory and research in mathematics education. Here we mention and explain briefly the key themes in the theory/research basis for our work.

Research From the Cognitive Sciences

1. **Social Constructivism** We are in general agreement with constructivist explanations of the ways that knowledge is developed, especially the social constructivist ideas about influence of discourse on learning. This position is reflected in the authors' decision to write materials that would support student-centered investigation of mathematical problems and in our attempt to design problem content and formats that would encourage student-student and student-teacher dialogue about the work.

2. **Conceptual and Procedural Knowledge** We have been influenced by theory and research indicating that mathematical understanding is fundamentally a web of logical and psychological connections among ideas. Furthermore, we have interpreted research on the interplay of conceptual and procedural knowledge to say that sound conceptual understanding is an important foundation for procedural skill, not an incidental and delayed consequence of repeated rote procedural practice.

3. **Multiple Representations** An important indication of students' connected mathematical knowledge is their ability to represent ideas in a variety of ways. We have interpreted this theory to imply that curriculum materials should frequently provide and ask for knowledge representation using graphs, number patterns, written explanations, and symbolic expressions.

4. **Cooperative Learning** There is a consistent and growing body of research indicating that when students engage in cooperative work on appropriate problem-solving tasks, their mathematical and social learning will be enhanced. We have interpreted this line of theory and research to imply that we should design student and teacher materials that are suitable for use in cooperative learning instructional formats as well as individual learning formats—the mathematical tasks dictate the format.

Research From Mathematics Education

5. **Rational Numbers/Proportional Reasoning** The extensive psychological literature on development of rational numbers and proportional reasoning has guided our development of curriculum materials addressing this important middle school topic. Furthermore, the implementation of CMP materials in real classrooms has allowed us to contribute to that literature with research

publications that show the effects of new teaching approaches to traditionally difficult topics.

6. Probability and Statistical Reasoning
The interesting research literature concerning development of and cognitive obstacles to student learning of statistical concepts, such as mean and graphic displays, and probability concepts, such as the law of large numbers and conditional probability, has been used as we developed the statistics and probability units of CMP materials.

7. Algebraic Reasoning The different conceptualizations of algebra described and researched in the literature contributed to the treatment of algebra in CMP. Various scholars describe algebra as a study of modeling, functions, generalized arithmetic, and/or as a problem-solving tool. CMP has aspects of each of these descriptions of algebra, but focuses more directly on functions and on the effects of rates of change on representations. The research literature illuminates some of the cognitive complexities inherent in algebraic reasoning and offers suggestions on helping students overcome difficulties. Research concerning concepts, such as equivalence, functions, the equal sign, algebraic variables, graphical representations, multiple representations, and the role of technology, were used as we developed the algebra units of the CMP materials.

8. Geometric/Measurement Reasoning
Results from national assessments and research findings show that student achievement in geometry and measurement is weak. Research on student understanding and learning of geometric/measurement concepts, such as angle, area, perimeter, volume, and processes such as visualization, contributed to the development of geometry/measurement units in CMP materials. As a result of research shifting from a focus on shape and form to the related ideas of congruence, similarity, and symmetry transformations, CMP geometry units were designed to focus on these important ideas.

Research From Education Policy and Organization

9. Motivation One of the fundamental challenges in mathematics teaching is convincing students that serious effort in study of the subject will be rewarding and that learning of mathematics can also be an enjoyable experience. We have paid careful attention to literature on extrinsic and intrinsic motivation, and we have done some informal developmental research of our own to discover aspects of mathematics and teaching that are most effective in engaging student attention and interest.

10. Teacher and School Change The most attractive school mathematics curriculum materials will be of little long-term value or effect if they are not put into use in schools. In the process of helping teachers through professional development, we have paid close attention to what is known about effective teacher professional development and the school strategies that seem to be most effective.

A good reference book to read for more insight into what research says in these areas is Kilpatrick, J., Martin, W.G., & Schifter, D. (Eds.) (2003) *A Research Companion to Principles and Standards for School Mathematics,* Reston, VA:NCTM. (ISBN 0-87353-537-5).

While each of these ten points indicates influence of theory and research on design and development of the CMP curriculum, teacher, and assessment materials, it would be misleading to suggest that the influence is direct and controlling in all decisions. As the authors have read the research literature reporting empirical and theoretical work, research findings and new ideas have been absorbed and factored into the creative, deliberative, and experimental process that leads to a comprehensive mathematics program for schools.

The authors were guided by the following principles in the development of the *Connected Mathematics* materials. These statements reflect both research and policy stances in mathematics education about what works to support students' learning of important mathematics.

- The "big" or key mathematical ideas around which the curriculum is built are identified.

- The underlying concepts, skills, or procedures supporting the development of a key idea are identified and included in an appropriate development sequence.

- An effective curriculum has coherence—it builds and connects from investigation to investigation, unit-to-unit, and grade-to-grade.

- Classroom instruction focuses on inquiry and investigation of mathematical ideas embedded in rich problem situations.

- Mathematical tasks for students in class and in homework are the primary vehicle for student engagement with the mathematical concepts to be learned. The key mathematical goals are elaborated, exemplified, and connected through the problems in an investigation.

- Ideas are explored through these tasks in the depth necessary to allow students to make sense of them. Superficial treatment of an idea produces shallow and short-lived understanding and does not support making connections among ideas.

- The curriculum helps students grow in their ability to reason effectively with information represented in graphic, numeric, symbolic, and verbal forms and to move flexibly among these representations.

- The curriculum reflects the information-processing capabilities of calculators and computers and the fundamental changes such tools are making in the way people learn mathematics and apply their knowledge of problem-solving tasks.

Connected Mathematics is different from many more familiar curricula in that it is problem centered. The following section elaborates what we mean by this and what the value added is for students of such a curriculum.

Rationale for a Problem-Centered Curriculum

Students' perceptions about a discipline come from the tasks or problems with which they are asked to engage. For example, if students in a geometry course are asked to memorize definitions, they think geometry is about memorizing definitions. If students spend a majority of their mathematics time practicing paper-and-pencil computations, they come to believe that mathematics is about calculating answers to arithmetic problems as quickly as possible. They may become faster at performing specific types of computations, but they may not be able to apply these skills to other situations or to recognize problems that call for these skills.

Formal mathematics begins with undefined terms, axioms, and definitions and deduces important conclusions logically from those starting points. However, mathematics is produced and used in a much more complex combination of exploration, experience-based intuition, and reflection. If the purpose of studying mathematics is to be able to solve a variety of problems, then students need to spend significant portions of their mathematics time solving problems that require thinking, planning, reasoning, computing, and evaluating.

A growing body of evidence from the cognitive sciences supports the theory that students can make sense of mathematics if the concepts and skills are embedded within a context or problem. If time is spent exploring interesting mathematics situations, reflecting on solution methods, examining why the methods work, comparing methods, and relating methods to those used in previous situations, then students are likely to build more robust understanding of mathematical concepts and related procedures. This method is quite different from the assumption that students learn by observing a teacher as he or she demonstrates how to solve a problem and then practices that method on similar problems.

A problem-centered curriculum not only helps students to make sense of the mathematics, it also helps them to process the mathematics in a retrievable way.

Teachers of CMP report that students in succeeding grades remember and refer to a concept, technique, or problem-solving strategy by the name of the problem in which they encountered the ideas. For example, the Basketball Problem from *What Do You Expect?* in Grade Seven becomes a trigger for remembering the processes of finding compound probabilities and expected values.

Results from the cognitive sciences also suggest that learning is enhanced if it is connected to prior knowledge and is more likely to be retained and applied to future learning. Critically examining, refining, and extending conjectures and strategies are also important aspects of becoming reflective learners.

In CMP, important mathematical ideas are embedded in the context of interesting problems. As students explore a series of connected problems, they develop understanding of the embedded ideas and, with the aid of the teacher, abstract powerful mathematical ideas, problem-solving strategies, and ways of thinking. They learn mathematics and learn how to learn mathematics.

Characteristics of Good Problems

To be effective, problems must embody critical concepts and skills and have the potential to engage students in making sense of mathematics. And, since students build understanding by reflecting, connecting, and communicating, the problems need to encourage them to use these processes.

Each problem in *Connected Mathematics* satisfies the following criteria:

- The problem must have important, useful mathematics embedded in it.

- Investigation of the problem should contribute to students' conceptual development of important mathematical ideas.

- Work on the problem should promote skillful use of mathematics and opportunities to practice important skills.

- The problem should create opportunities for teachers to assess what students are learning and where they are experiencing difficulty.

In addition each problem satisfies some or all of the following criteria:

- The problem should engage students and encourage classroom discourse.

- The problem should allow various solution strategies or lead to alternative decisions that can be taken and defended.

- Solution of the problem should require higher-level thinking and problem solving.

- The mathematical content of the problem should connect to other important mathematical ideas.

Practice With Concepts, Related Skills, and Algorithms

Students need to practice mathematical concepts, ideas, and procedures to reach a level of fluency that allows them to "think" with the ideas in new situations. To accomplish this we were guided by the following principles related to skills practice.

- Immediate practice should be related to the situations in which the ideas have been developed and learned.

- Continued practice should use skills and procedures in situations that connect to ideas that students have already encountered.

- Students need opportunities to use the ideas and skills in situations that extend beyond familiar situations. These opportunities allow students to use skills and concepts in new combinations to solve new kinds of problems.

- Students need practice distributed over time to allow high ideas, concepts and procedures to reach a level of fluency of use in familiar and unfamiliar situations and to build connections to other concepts and procedures.

- Students need guidance in reflecting on what they are learning, how the ideas fit together, and how to make judgments about what is helpful in which kinds of situations.

- Throughout the Number and Algebra Strands development, students need to learn how to make judgments about what operation or combination of operations or representations is useful in a given situation, as well as, how to become skillful at carrying out the needed computation(s). Knowing how to, but not when to, is insufficient.

Rationale for Depth versus Spiraling

The concept of a "spiraling" curriculum is philosophically appealing; but, too often, not enough time is spent initially with a new concept to build on it at the next stage of the spiral. This leads to teachers spending a great deal of time re-teaching the same ideas over and over again. Without a deeper understanding of concepts and how they are connected, students come to view mathematics as a collection of different techniques and algorithms to be memorized.

Problem solving based on such learning becomes a search for the correct algorithm rather than seeking to make sense of the situation, considering the nature and size of a solution, putting together a solution path that makes sense, and examining the solution in light of the original question. Taking time to allow the ideas studied to be more carefully developed means that when these ideas are met in future units, students have a solid foundation on which to build. Rather than being caught in a cycle of relearning the same ideas superficially which are quickly forgotten, students are able to connect new ideas to previously learned ideas and make substantive advances in knowledge.

With any important mathematical concept, there are many related ideas, procedures, and skills. At each grade level, a small, select set of important mathematical concepts, ideas, and related procedures are studied in depth rather than skimming through a larger set of ideas in a shallow manner. This means that time is allocated to develop understanding of key ideas in contrast to "covering" a book. The Teacher's Guides accompanying CMP materials were developed to support teachers in planning for and teaching a problem-centered curriculum. Practice on related skills and algorithms are provided in a distributed fashion so that students not only practice these skills and algorithms to reach facility in carrying out computations, but they also learn to put their growing body of skills together to solve new problems.

Developing Depth of Understanding and Use

Through the field trials process we were able to develop units that result in student understanding of key ideas in depth. An example is illustrated in the way that *Connected Mathematics* treats proportional reasoning—a fundamentally important topic for middle school mathematics and beyond. Conventional treatments of this central topic are often limited to a brief expository presentation of the ideas of ratio and proportion, followed by training in techniques for solving proportions. In contrast, the CMP curriculum materials develop core elements of proportional reasoning in a seventh grade unit, *Comparing and Scaling,* with the groundwork for this unit having been developed in four prior units. Five succeeding units build on and connect to students' understanding of proportional reasoning. These units and their connections are summarized as follows:

Grade 6 *Bits and Pieces I* and *II* introduce students to fractions and their various meanings and uses. Models for making sense of fraction meanings and of operating with fractions are introduced and used. These early experiences include fractions as ratios. The extensive work with equivalent forms of fractions builds the skills needed to work with ratio and proportion problems. These ideas are developed further in the probability unit *How Likely Is It?* in which ratio comparisons are informally used to compare probabilities. For example, is the probability of drawing a green block from a bag the same if we have 10 green and 15 red or 20 green and 30 red?

Grade 7 *Stretching and Shrinking* introduces proportionality concepts in the context of geometric problems involving similarity. Students connect visual ideas of enlarging and reducing figures, numerical ideas of scale factors and ratios, and applications of similarity through work with problems focused around the question: "What would it mean to say two figures are similar?"

The next unit in grade seven is the core proportional reasoning unit, *Comparing and Scaling,* which connects fractions, percents, and ratios through investigation of various situations in which the central question is: "What strategies make sense in describing how much greater one quantity is than another?" Through a series of problem-based investigations, students explore the meaning of ratio comparison and develop, in a progression from intuition to articulate procedures, a variety of techniques for dealing with such questions.

A seventh grade unit that follows, *Moving Straight Ahead,* is a unit on linear relationships and equations. Proportional thinking is connected and extended to the core ideas of linearity—constant rate of change and slope. Then in the probability unit *What Do You Expect?,* students again use ratios to make comparisons of probabilities.

Grade 8 *Thinking With Mathematical Models*; *Looking For Pythagoras; Growing, Growing, Growing,* and *Frogs, Fleas,* and *Painted Cubes* extend the understanding of proportional relationships by investigating the contrast between linear relationships and inverse, exponential, and quadratic relationships. Also in Grade Eight, *Samples and Populations* uses proportional reasoning in comparing data situations and in choosing samples from populations.

These unit descriptions show two things about *Connected Mathematics*—the in-depth development of fundamental ideas and the connected use of these important ideas throughout the rest of the units.

Support for Classroom Teachers

When mathematical ideas are embedded in problem-based investigations of rich context, the teacher has a critical responsibility for ensuring that students abstract and generalize the important mathematical concepts and procedures from the experiences with the problems. In a problem-centered classroom, teachers take on new roles—moving from always being the one who does the mathematics to being the one who guides, interrogates, and facilitates the learner in doing and making sense of the mathematics.

The Teacher's Guides and Assessment Resources developed for *Connected Mathematics* provide these kinds of help for the teacher:

- The Teacher's Guide for each unit engages teachers in a conversation about what is possible in the classroom around a particular lesson. Goals for each lesson are articulated. Suggestions are made about how to engage the students in the mathematics task, how to

promote student thinking and reasoning during the exploration of the problem, and how to summarize with the students the important mathematics embedded in the problem. Support for this Launch—Explore—Summarize sequence occurs for each problem in the CMP curriculum.

- An overview and elaboration of the mathematics of the unit is located at the beginning of each Teacher's Guide, along with examples and a rationale for the models and procedures used. This mathematical essay helps a teacher stand above the unit and see the mathematics from a perspective that includes the particular unit, connects to earlier units, and projects to where the mathematics goes in subsequent units and years.

- Actual classroom scenarios are included to help stimulate teachers' imaginations about what is possible.

- Questions to ask students at all stages of the lesson are included to help teachers support student learning.

- Reflections questions are provided at the end of each investigation to help teachers assess what sense students are making of the 'big" ideas and to help students abstract, generalize, and record the mathematical ideas and techniques developed in the Investigation.

- Diverse kinds of assessments are included in the student units and the Assessment Resources that mirror classroom practices as well as highlight important concepts, skills, techniques, and problem solving strategies.

- Multiple kinds of assessment are included to help teachers see assessment and evaluation as a way to inform students of their progress, apprise parents of students' progress, and guide the decisions a teacher makes about lesson plans and classroom interactions.

See pages 73–77 for more details about teacher support materials.

Research, Field Testing, and Evaluation

Before starting the design phase of the materials, we commissioned individual reviews of the first edition of CMP units from 84 individuals in 17 states and comprehensive reviews from more than 20 schools in 14 states.

Individual Reviews These reviews focused on particular strands over all three grades (such as number, algebra, or statistics) on particular sub-populations (such as students with special needs or students who are commonly underserved), or on topical concerns (such as language use and readability).

Comprehensive Reviews These reviews were conducted in groups that included teachers, administrators, curriculum supervisors, mathematicians, experts in special education, language, and reading level analyses, English language learners, issues of equity, and others. Each group reviewed an entire grade level of the curriculum. All responses were coded and entered into a database that allowed reports to be printed for any issue or combination of issues that would be helpful to an author or staff person in designing a unit.

In addition, CMP issued a call to schools to serve as pilot schools for the development of CMP2. We received 50 applications from districts for piloting. From these applications we chose 15 that included 49 school sites in 12 states and the District of Columbia. We received evaluation feedback from these sites over the five-year cycle of development.

Based on the commissioned reviews, what the authors had learned from CMP schools over a 6-year period, and input from our Advisory Board, the authors started with grades 6 and 7 and systematically revised and restructured the units and their sequence for each grade-level to create a first draft of the revision. These were sent to our pilot schools to be taught during the second year of the project. These initial grade level unit drafts were the basis for substantial feedback from our trial teachers.

Examples of the kinds of questions we asked the trial teachers following each iteration of a unit or grade level are given below.

"BIG PICTURE" UNIT FEEDBACK

1. Is the mathematics of the unit important for students at this grade level? Explain.

2. Are the mathematical goals of the unit clear to you?

3. Overall, what are the strengths and weaknesses in this unit?

4. Please comment on your students' achievement of mathematics understanding at the end of this unit. What concepts/skills did they "nail"? Which concepts/skills are still developing? Which concepts/skills need a great deal more reinforcement?

5. Is there a flow to the sequencing of the Investigations? Does the mathematics develop smoothly throughout the unit? Are there any big leaps where another problem is needed to help students understand a big idea in an Investigation? What adjustments did you make in these rough spots?

PROBLEM-BY-PROBLEM FEEDBACK

1. Are the mathematical goals of each problem/investigation clear to you?

2. Is the language and wording of each problem understandable to students?

3. Are there any grammatical or mathematical errors in the problems? (Please be as specific as possible.)

4. Are there any problems that you think can be deleted?

5. Are there any problems that needed serious revision?

APPLICATIONS•CONNECTIONS•EXTENSIONS FEEDBACK

1. Does the format of the ACE exercises work for you and your students? Why or why not?

2. Which ACE exercises work well, which would you change, and why?

3. What needs to be added to or deleted from the ACE exercises? Is there enough practice for

students? How do you supplement and why?

4. Are there sufficient ACE exercises that challenge your more interested and capable students? If not, what needs to be added and why?

5. Are there sufficient ACE exercises that are accessible to and helpful to students that need more scaffolding for the mathematical ideas?

MATHEMATICAL REFLECTIONS AND LOOKING BACK, LOOKING AHEAD FEEDBACK

1. Are these reflections useful to you and your students in identifying and making more explicit the "big" mathematical ideas in the unit? If not, how could they be improved?

ASSESSMENT MATERIALS FEEDBACK

1. Are the check-ups, quizzes, unit tests, and projects useful to you? If not, how can they be improved? What should be deleted and what should be added? (Please give specifics.)

2. How do you use the assessment materials? Do you supplement the materials? If so, how and why?

TEACHER'S GUIDE FEEDBACK

1. Is the Teacher's Guide useful to you? If not, what changes do you suggest and why?

2. Which parts of the Teacher's Guide help you and which do you ignore or seldom use?

3. What would be helpful to add or expand in the Teacher's Guide?

YEAR-END GRADE LEVEL FEEDBACK

1. Are the mathematical concepts, skills and processes in the units appropriate for the grade level?

2. Is the grade level placement of units optimal for your school district? Why or why not?

3. Does the mathematics flow smoothly for the students over the year?

4. Once an idea is learned, is there sufficient reinforcement and use in succeeding units?

5. Are connections made between units within the grade level?

6. Does the grade level sequence of units seem appropriate? If not, what changes would you make and why?

7. Overall, what are the strengths and weaknesses in the units for the year? (Please be as specific as possible.)

BIG PICTURE QUESTION

1. What three to five things would you have us seriously improve, change, or drop at each grade level? Please be specific about exactly what you suggest and why you would like to see this change.

Development Summary

CMP development followed the very rigorous design, field-test, evaluate loop pictured in the

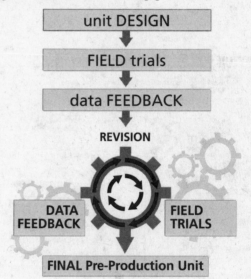

diagram below.

The units for each grade level went through at least three cycles of field trials–data feedback– revision. If needed, units had four rounds of field trials. This process of (1) commissioning reviews from experts, (2) using the field trials– feedback loops for the materials, (3) conducting key classroom observations by the CMP staff of units being taught, and (4) monitoring student performance on state and local tests by trial schools comprises research-based development of curriculum. This process takes five years to produce the final drafts of units that are sent to the publisher. Another 6 to 18 months is needed for editing, design, and layout for the published units. This process produces materials that are cohesive and effectively sequenced.

An Example of Effective Sequencing of Problems

To be effective, problems must be carefully sequenced to help students develop appropriate understanding and skill. The following set of problems from the Grade 6 unit, *Covering and Surrounding,* develops methods for finding the circumference and area of a circle.

The first problem uses the context of irregularly–shaped lakes to explore possible relationships between the perimeter of a curved figure and its area. Using a square grid to estimate perimeter and area helps students to understand the meaning of perimeter and area before using formulas.

In the second problem, students measure the diameter and circumference of several circular objects. They create a table and a graph of their data and look for a pattern relating the two measurements. Students should discover that the circumference is the diameter times "a little bit more than 3." With the help of the teacher, students are introduced to the idea of pi or π and find a closer approximation of its value.

Covering and Surrounding • page 73

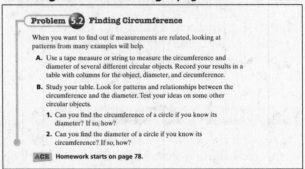

Problem 5.2 Finding Circumference

When you want to find out if measurements are related, looking at patterns from many examples will help.

  A. Use a tape measure or string to measure the circumference and diameter of several different circular objects. Record your results in a table with columns for the object, diameter, and circumference.

  B. Study your table. Look for patterns and relationships between the circumference and the diameter. Test your ideas on some other circular objects.

   1. Can you find the circumference of a circle if you know its diameter? If so, how?

   2. Can you find the diameter of a circle if you know its circumference? If so, how?

ACE Homework starts on page 78.

The third problem asks students to estimate the area of a circle. Students are encouraged to think of several different methods and to explain their thinking. This problem is intended to motivate the need for a shortcut for calculating the area. To answer Parts C and D, students must consider the relationships between each of the measurements—radius, diameter, circumference, and area—and the possible price of each pizza.

Covering and Surrounding • page 71

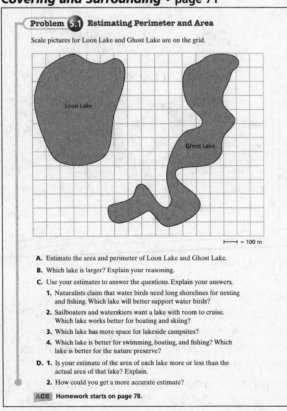

Problem 5.1 Estimating Perimeter and Area

Scale pictures for Loon Lake and Ghost Lake are on the grid.

⊢—⊣ = 100 m

  A. Estimate the area and perimeter of Loon Lake and Ghost Lake.

  B. Which lake is larger? Explain your reasoning.

  C. Use your estimates to answer the questions. Explain your answers.

   1. Naturalists claim that water birds need long shorelines for nesting and fishing. Which lake will better support water birds?

   2. Sailboaters and waterskiers want a lake with room to cruise. Which lake works better for boating and skiing?

   3. Which lake has more space for lakeside campsites?

   4. Which lake is better for swimming, boating, and fishing? Which lake is better for the nature preserve?

  D. 1. Is your estimate of the area of each lake more or less than the actual area of that lake? Explain.

   2. How could you get a more accurate estimate?

ACE Homework starts on page 78.

Covering and Surrounding • page 75

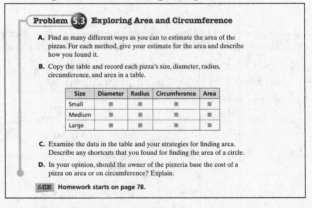

Problem 5.3 Exploring Area and Circumference

  A. Find as many different ways as you can to estimate the area of the pizzas. For each method, give your estimate for the area and describe how you found it.

  B. Copy the table and record each pizza's size, diameter, radius, circumference, and area in a table.

Size	Diameter	Radius	Circumference	Area
Small	▨	▨	▨	▨
Medium	▨	▨	▨	▨
Large	▨	▨	▨	▨

  C. Examine the data in the table and your strategies for finding area. Describe any shortcuts that you found for finding the area of a circle.

  D. In your opinion, should the owner of the pizzeria base the cost of a pizza on area or on circumference? Explain.

ACE Homework starts on page 78.

In the fourth problem, students estimate the number of "radius squares" (squares with side length equal to the radius of the circle) it takes to cover a circle. This problem helps students discover the formula for the area of a circle and to understand why it makes sense. Students should find that the area of a circle is "a little bit more than 3" radius squares. With the help of the teachers, students relate "a little bit more than 3" to the number π, and develop the area formula $A = \pi \cdot r^2$. Mental images such as the square embedded in a circle trigger a way for students to recall the formula for the area of a circle and to remember why the formula makes sense.

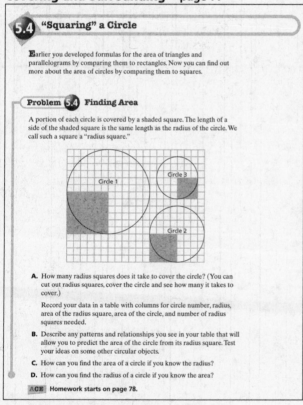

Covering and Surrounding • page 77

5.4 "Squaring" a Circle

Earlier you developed formulas for the area of triangles and parallelograms by comparing them to rectangles. Now you can find out more about the area of circles by comparing them to squares.

Problem **5.4** Finding Area

A portion of each circle is covered by a shaded square. The length of a side of the shaded square is the same length as the radius of the circle. We call such a square a "radius square."

A. How many radius squares does it take to cover the circle? (You can cut out radius squares, cover the circle and see how many it takes to cover.)

Record your data in a table with columns for circle number, radius, area of the radius square, area of the circle, and number of radius squares needed.

B. Describe any patterns and relationships you see in your table that will allow you to predict the area of the circle from its radius square. Test your ideas on some other circular objects.

C. How can you find the area of a circle if you know the radius?

D. How can you find the radius of a circle if you know the area?

ACE Homework starts on page 78.

The sequencing of this set of problems and its effectiveness is reflective of the interactions between the authors and the teachers and students at our trial sites.

CMP: A Curriculum Co-Developed With Teachers and Students

Developing a curriculum with a complex set of interrelated goals takes time and input from many people. As authors, our work was based on a set of deep commitments we had about what would constitute a more powerful way to engage students in making sense of mathematics. Our Advisory Board took an active role in reading and critiquing units in their various iterations. In order to enact our development principles, we found that three full years of field trials in schools was essential for each year of the materials. This feedback from teachers and students across the country is the key element in the success of the *Connected Mathematics Project* materials. The final materials comprised the ideas that stood the test of time in classrooms across the country. Nearly 200 teachers in 15 trial sites around the country (and their thousands of students) are a significant part of the team of professionals that made these materials happen. The scenarios of teacher and student interactions with the materials became the most compelling parts of the Teacher's Guides.

Without the bravery of these teachers in using materials that were never perfect in their first versions, CMP would have been a set of ideas that lived in the brains and imaginations of the five authors. Instead, they are materials with classroom heart because our trial teachers and students made them so. We believe that such materials have the potential to dramatically change what students know and are able to do in mathematical situations. The emphasis on thinking and reasoning, on making sense of ideas, on making students responsible for both having and explaining their ideas, on developing sound mathematics habits gives students opportunities to learn in ways that can change how they think of themselves as learners of mathematics.

From the authors' perspectives, our hope is to develop materials that play out deeply held beliefs and firmly grounded theories about what mathematics is important for students to learn and how they should learn it. We hope that we have been a part of helping to challenge and change the curriculum landscape of our country. Our students are worth the effort.

Mathematics Content of CMP2

The mathematical content developed in *Connected Mathematics* covers number, geometry, measurement, statistics, probability, and algebra appropriate for the middle grades.

Connected Mathematics 2 provides 24 units (8 at each grade level). Three additional units continue to be available from the first edition of *Connected Mathematics* to meet specific state or local needs (1 at each grade level). Every unit develops a "big mathematical idea," that is, an important cluster of related concepts, skills, procedures, and ways of thinking. The following table gives an overview of the curriculum at each grade level.

Contents in Brief, by Unit

Grade 6	Grade 7	Grade 8
Prime Time *Factors and Multiples* number theory, including factors, multiples, primes, composites, prime factorization	**Variables and Patterns** *Introducing Algebra* variables; representations of relationships, including tables, graphs, words, and symbols	**Thinking With Mathematical Models** *Linear and Inverse Variation* introduction to functions and modeling; finding the equation of a line; inverse functions; inequalities
Bits and Pieces I *Understanding Rational Numbers* move among fractions, decimals, and percents; compare and order rational numbers; equivalence	**Stretching and Shrinking** *Similarity* similar figures; scale factors; side length ratios; basic similarity transformations and their algebraic rules	**Looking for Pythagoras** *The Pythagorean Theorem* square roots; the Pythagorean Theorem; connections among coordinates, slope, distance, and area; distances in the plane
Shapes and Designs *Two-Dimensional Geometry* regular and non-regular polygons, special properties of triangles and quadrilaterals, angle measure, angle sums, tiling, the triangle inequality	**Comparing and Scaling** *Ratio, Proportion, and Percent* rates and ratios; making comparisons; proportional reasoning; solving proportions	**Growing, Growing, Growing** *Exponential Relationships* recognize and represent exponential growth and decay in tables, graphs, words, and symbols; rules of exponents; scientific notation
Bits and Pieces II *Understanding Fraction Operations* understanding and skill with addition, subtraction, multiplication, and division of fractions	**Accentuate the Negative** *Positive and Negative Numbers* understanding and modeling positive and negative integers and rational numbers; operations; order of operations; distributive property; four-quadrant graphing	**Frogs, Fleas and Painted Cubes** *Quadratic Relationships* recognize and represent quadratic functions in tables, graphs, words and symbols; factor simple quadratic expressions
Covering and Surrounding *Two-Dimensional Measurement* area and perimeter relationships, including minima and maxima; area and perimeter of polygons and circles, including formulas	**Moving Straight Ahead** *Linear Relationships* recognize and represent linear relationships in tables, graphs, words, and symbols; solve linear equations; slope	**Kaleidoscopes, Hubcaps and Mirrors** *Symmetry and Transformations* symmetries of designs, symmetry transformations, congruence, congruence rules for triangles
Bits and Pieces III *Computing With Decimals and Percents* understanding and skill with addition, subtraction, multiplication, and division of decimals, solving percent problems	**Filling and Wrapping** *Three-Dimensional Measurement* spatial visualization, volume and surface area of various solids, volume and surface area relationship	**Say It With Symbols** *Making Sense of Symbols* equivalent expressions, substitute and combine expressions, solve quadratic equations, the quadratic formula
How Likely Is It? *Probability* reason about uncertainty, calculate experimental and theoretical probabilities, equally-likely and non-equally-likely outcomes	**What Do You Expect?** *Probability and Expected Value* expected value, probabilities of two-stage outcomes	**Shapes of Algebra** *Linear Systems and Inequalities* coordinate geometry, solve inequalities, standard form of linear equations, solve systems of linear equations and linear inequalities
Data About Us *Statistics* formulate questions; gather, organize, represent, and analyze data; interpret results from data; measures of center and range	**Data Distributions** *Describing Variability and Comparing Groups* measures of center, variability in data, comparing distributions of equal and unequal sizes	**Samples and Populations** *Data and Statistics* use samples to reason about populations and make predictions, compare samples and sample distributions, relationships among attributes in data sets

Mathematics Learning Goals

Connected *Mathematics* develops four mathematical strands: Number and Operation, Geometry and Measurement, Data Analysis and Probability, and Algebra. The mathematical learning goals below signify what students should be able to do by the end of eighth grade in each strand. Beside each bulleted goal is a reference to the grade level (6, 7 or 8) when the specific content is covered. It is important to note that many of the goals are revisited in later units many times, either within classroom Problems or in the Connections Problems in the ACE homework assignments. For example, the bulleted goal under Number Sense of "Express rational numbers in equivalent forms" is labeled a Grade 6 goal because the unit *Bits and Pieces I* includes this goal as a "big idea". However, practice with this goal occurs throughout the curriculum.

Goals by Mathematics Strand

NUMBER AND OPERATION GOALS

Number Sense

- Use numbers in various forms to solve problems (6, 7, 8)

- Understand and use large numbers, including in exponential and scientific notation (6, 7, 8)

- Reason proportionally in a variety of contexts using geometric and numerical reasoning, including scaling and solving proportions (6, 7, 8)

- Compare numbers in a variety of ways, including differences, rates, ratios, and percents and choose when each comparison is appropriate (6, 7, 8)

- Order positive and/or negative rational numbers (6, 7, 8)

- Express rational numbers in equivalent forms (6)

- Make estimates and use benchmarks (6, 7, 8)

Operations and Algorithms

- Develop understanding and skill with all four arithmetic operations on fractions and decimals (6)

- Develop understanding and skill in solving a variety of percent problems (6)

- Use the order of operations to write, evaluate, and simplify numerical expressions (7, 8)

- Develop fluency with paper and pencil computation, calculator use, mental calculation, and estimation; and choose among these when solving problems (6, 7)

Properties

- Understand the multiplicative structure of numbers, including the concepts of prime and composite numbers, evens, odds, and prime factorizations (6)

- Use the commutative and distributive properties to write equivalent numerical expressions (7, 8)

DATA AND PROBABILITY GOALS

Formulating Questions

- Formulate questions that can be answered through data collection and analysis (6, 7, 8)

- Design data collection strategies to gather data to answer these questions (6, 7, 8)

- Design experiments and simulations to test hypotheses about probability situations (8)

Data Collection

- Carry out data collection strategies to answer questions (6, 7, 8)

- Distinguish between samples and populations (8)

- Characterize samples as representative or non-representative, as random (8)

- Use these characterizations to evaluate the quality of the collected data (8)

Data Analysis

- Organize, analyze, and interpret data to make predictions, construct arguments, and make decisions (6, 7)

- Use measures of center and spread to describe and to compare data sets (6, 7)

- Be able to read, create, and choose data representations, including bar graphs, line plots, coordinate graphs, box and whisker plots, histograms, and stem and leaf plots (6, 7)

- Informally evaluate the significance of differences between sets of data (7, 8)

- Use information from samples to draw conclusions about populations (8)

Probability

- Distinguish between theoretical and experimental probabilities and understand the relationship between them (6)

- Use probability concepts to make decisions (6)

- Find and interpret expected value (7)

- Compute and compare the chances of various outcomes, including two-stage outcomes (7)

GEOMETRY AND MEASUREMENT GOALS

Shapes and Their Properties

- Generate important examples of angles, lines, and two- and three-dimensional shapes (6)

- Categorize, define, and relate figures in a variety of representations (6, 7)

- Understand principles governing the construction of shapes with reasons why certain shapes serve special purposes (e.g. triangles for trusses) (6)

- Build and visualize three-dimensional figures from various two-dimensional representations and vice versa (7)

- Recognize and use shapes and their properties to make mathematical arguments and to solve problems (6, 7, 8)

- Use the Pythagorean Theorem and properties of special triangles (e.g. isosceles right triangles) to solve problems (8)

- Use a coordinate grid to describe and investigate relationships among shapes (7, 8)

- Recognize and use standard, essential geometric vocabulary (6, 7, 8)

Transformations—Symmetry, Similarity, and Congruence

- Recognize line, rotational, and translational symmetries and use them to solve problems (6, 8)

- Use scale factor and ratios to create similar figures or determine whether two or more shapes are similar or congruent (7)

- Predict ways that similarity and congruence transformations affect lengths, angle measures, perimeters, areas, volume, and orientation (7, 8)

- Investigate the effects of combining one or more transformations of a shape (8)

- Identify and use congruent triangles and/or quadrilaterals to solve problems about shapes and measurement (6, 8)

- Use properties of similar figures to solve problems about shapes and measurement (7)

- Use a coordinate grid to explore and verify similarity and congruence relationships (7, 8)

Measurement

- Understand what it means to measure an attribute of a figure or a phenomenon (6)

- Estimate and measure angles, line segments, areas, and volumes using tools and formulas (6, 7)

- Relate angle measure and side lengths to the shape of a polygon (6)

- Find area and perimeter of rectangles, parallelograms, triangles, circles, and irregular figures (7)

- Find surface area and volume of rectangular solids, cylinders, prisms, cones, and pyramids and the volume of spheres (7)

- Relate units within and between the customary and metric systems (6, 7)

- Use ratios and proportions to derive indirect measurements (7)

- Use measurement concepts to solve problems (6, 7, 8)

Geometric Connections

- Use geometric concepts to build understanding of concepts in other areas of mathematics (6, 7, 8)

- Connect geometric concepts to concepts in other areas of mathematics (6, 7, 8)

Patterns of Change—Functions

- Identify and use variables to describe relationships between quantitative variables in order to solve problems or make decisions (7, 8)

- Recognize and distinguish among patterns of change associated with linear, inverse, exponential and quadratic functions (7, 8)

Representation

- Construct tables, graphs, symbolic expressions and verbal descriptions and use them to describe and predict patterns of change in variables (7, 8)

- Move easily among tables, graphs, symbolic expressions, and verbal descriptions (7, 8)

- Describe the advantages and disadvantages of each representation and use these descriptions to make choices when solving problems (7, 8)

- Use linear, inverse, exponential, and quadratic equations and inequalities as mathematical models of situations involving variables (7, 8)

Symbolic Reasoning

- Connect equations to problem situations (7, 8)

- Connect solving equations in one variable to finding specific values of functions (8)

- Solve linear equations and inequalities and simple quadratic equations using symbolic methods (7, 8)

- Find equivalent forms of many kinds of equations, including factoring simple quadratic equations (7, 8)

- Use the distributive and commutative properties to write equivalent expressions and equations (8)

- Solve systems of linear equations (8)

- Solve systems of linear inequalities by graphing (8)

Content Goals in Each Unit

Connected Mathematics 2 provides eight student units for each grade level. Each unit is organized around an important mathematical idea or cluster of related ideas as described in the table on page 15. Each unit covers material in a particular strand of mathematics. This classification by strand is meant to highlight the strand that is the primary focus of the unit. However, there are problems in every unit that connect to the other three strands. For example, the unit *Shapes of Algebra* is classified under Algebra. Even though this unit's focus is primarily on algebraic ideas, there are many connections to geometry, as the unit's name implies.

UNITS ORGANIZED BY STRAND

Number

Prime Time (Grade 6)

Bits and Pieces I (Grade 6)

Bits and Pieces II (Grade 6)

Bits and Pieces III (Grade 6)

Comparing and Scaling (Grade 7)

Accentuate the Negative (Grade 7)

Geometry

Shapes and Designs (Grade 6)

Covering and Surrounding (Grade 6)

Stretching and Shrinking (Grade 7)

Filling and Wrapping (Grade 7)

Looking of Pythagoras (Grade 8)

Kaleidoscopes, Hubcaps, and Mirrors (Grade 8)

Algebra

Variables and Patterns (Grade 7)

Moving Straight Ahead (Grade 7)

Thinking With Mathematical Models (Grade 8)

Growing, Growing, Growing (Grade 8)

Frogs, Fleas, and Painted Cubes (Grade 8)

Say It With Symbols (Grade 8)

Shapes of Algebra (Grade 8)

Data Analysis and Probability

How Likely Is It? (Grade 6)

Data About Us (Grade 6)

What Do You Expect? (Grade 7)

Data Distributions (Grade 7)

Samples and Populations (Grade 8)

In order to have a clearer idea of the particular goals for each unit, the goals are listed below by unit name. The units are sequenced in the order they are intended to be taught.

The ninth unit at each grade level, available from the first edition of CMP, can be used as a stand-alone unit for various purposes. For example, the unit *Ruins of Montarek* has been taught at Grade 5, as well as in art classes and social studies classes. Depending on your state or local standards, parts or all of these three additional units can be supplemented into the curriculum. The goals of each supplemental unit are listed below, after the CMP2 units.

Some questions to ask yourself as you examine the list of unit goals that follow:

- *How does a particular strand play out? For example, how are the number units sequenced? What units in each grade are in the number strand? How do the number systems with which students work grow as the curriculum progresses (ie, whole numbers, fractions, decimals, irrational numbers)*

- *When following a key goal for a unit: Does a later unit further develop this same goal and if so how?*

- *What goals have my students already met from prior units? What prior knowledge do they have that I can draw on?*

- *How does a concept grow? For example, which units are setting the groundwork for linear functions? What units cover this topic and how does this idea grow in complexity?*

- *Why are the units from different strands interspersed? What connections are made between the strands, between the units within a grade level, between the units in different grade levels?*

GRADE SIX GOALS

Prime Time (Number)

- Understand relationships among factors, multiples, divisors, and products

- Recognize and use properties of prime and composite numbers, even and odd numbers, and square numbers

- Use rectangles to represent the factor pairs of numbers

- Develop strategies for finding factors and multiples, least common multiples, and greatest common factors

- Recognize and use the fact that every whole number greater than 1 can be written in exactly one way as a product of prime numbers

- Use factors and multiples to solve problems and to explain some numerical facts of everyday life

- Develop a variety of strategies for solving problems—building models, making lists and tables, drawing diagrams, and solving simpler problems

Bits and Pieces I (Number)

- Build an understanding of fractions, decimals, and percents and the relationships between and among these concepts and their representations

- Develop ways to model situations involving fractions, decimals, and percents

- Understand and use equivalent fractions to reason about situations

- Compare and order fractions

- Move flexibly among fraction, decimal, and percent representations

- Use benchmarks such as 0, 1/2 and 1 to help estimate the size of a number or sum

- Develop and use benchmarks that relate different forms of representations of rational numbers (for example, 50% can be represented as 0.5)

- Use physical models and drawings to help reason about a situation

- Look for patterns and describe how to continue the pattern

- Use context to help reason about a situation

- Use estimation to understand a situation

Shapes and Designs (Geometry)

- Understand some important properties of polygons and recognize polygonal shapes both in and out of the classroom

- Investigate the symmetries of a shape— rotational or reflectional

- Estimate the size of any angle using reference to a right angle and other benchmark angles

- Use an angle ruler for making more accurate angle measurements

- Explore parallel lines and angles created by lines intersecting parallel lines

- Find patterns that help determine angle sums of polygons
- Determine which polygons fit together to cover a flat surface and why
- Explain the property of triangles that makes them useful as a stable structure for building
- Find that the sum of any two side lengths of a triangle is greater than the third side length
- Find that the sum of any three side lengths of a quadrilateral is greater than the fourth side length
- Reason about and solve problems involving shapes

Bits and Pieces II (Number)

- Use benchmarks and other strategies to estimate the reasonableness of results of operations with fractions
- Develop ways to model sums, differences, products, and quotients with areas, strips, and number lines
- Use estimates and exact solutions to make decisions
- Look for and generalize patterns in numbers
- Use knowledge of fractions and equivalence of fractions to develop algorithms for adding, subtracting, multiplying and dividing fractions
- Recognize when addition, subtraction, multiplication, or division is the appropriate operation to solve a problem
- Write fact families to show the inverse relationship between addition and subtraction, and between multiplication and division
- Solve problems using arithmetic operations on fractions

Covering and Surrounding (Geometry)

- Understand area and relate area to covering a figure
- Understand perimeter and relate perimeter to surrounding a figure
- Develop strategies for finding areas and perimeters of rectangular shapes and non-rectangular shapes
- Discover relationships between perimeter and area. including that each can vary while the other stays fixed
- Understand how the areas of simple geometric figures relate to each other (e.g. the area of a

parallelogram is twice the area of a triangle with the same base and height)
- Develop formulas and procedures—stated in words and/or symbols—for finding areas and perimeters of rectangles, parallelograms, triangles, and circles
- Develop techniques for estimating the area and perimeter of an irregular figure
- Recognize situations in which measuring perimeter or area will help answer practical questions

Bits and Pieces III (Number)

- Build on knowledge of operations on fractions and whole numbers
- Develop and use benchmarks and other strategies to estimate the answers to computations with decimals
- Develop meaning of and algorithms for operations with decimals
- Use the relationship between decimals and fractions to develop and understand why decimal algorithms work
- Use the place value interpretation of decimals to make sense of short-cut algorithms for operations
- Generalize number patterns to help make sense of decimal operations
- Choose between addition, subtraction, multiplication or division as an appropriate operation to use to solve a problem
- Understand that decimals are often associated with measurements in real world situations
- Solve problems using operations on decimals
- Use understanding of operations and the meaning of percents to solve percent problems of the form $a\%$ of b equals c for any one of the variables a, b, or c
- Create and interpret circle graphs

How Likely Is It? (Probability)

- Understand that probabilities are useful for predicting what will happen over the long run
- Understand the concepts of equally likely and not-equally likely
- Understand that fairness implies equally likely outcomes

- Understand that there are two ways to build probability models: by gathering data from experiments (experimental probability) and by analyzing the possible equally likely outcomes (theoretical probability)

- Understand that experimental probabilities are better estimates of theoretical probabilities when they are based on larger numbers of trials

- Develop strategies for finding both experimental and theoretical probabilities

- Critically interpret statements of probability to make decisions or answer questions

Data About Us (Data Analysis)

- Understand and use the process of data investigation by posing questions, collecting data, analyzing data distributions, and making interpretations to answer questions

- Represent data distributions using line plots, bar graphs, stem-and-leaf plots, and coordinate graphs

- Compute the mean, median, or mode and the range of the data

- Distinguish between categorical data and numerical data and identify which graphs and statistics may be used to represent each kind of data

- Make informed decisions about which graph or graphs and which of the measures of center (mean, median, or mode) and range may be used to describe a data distribution

- Develop strategies for comparing data distributions

Ruins of Montarek (Geometry)
Available in first edition ©2004.

- Read and make two-dimensional representations of three-dimensional cube buildings

- Observe that the back view of a cube building is the mirror image of the front view and that the left view is the mirror image of the right view

- Explain how drawings of the base outline, front view, and right view describe a building

- Construct cube buildings that fit two-dimensional building plans

- Develop a way to describe all buildings that can be made from a set of plans

- Understand that a set of plans can have more than one minimal building but only one maximal building

- Explain how a cube can be represented on isometric dot paper, how the angles on the cube are represented with angles on the dot paper, and how the representations fit what the eye sees when viewing the corner of a cube building

- Make isometric drawings of cube buildings

- Visualize transformations of cube buildings and make isometric drawings of the transformed buildings

- Reason about spatial relationships

- Use models and representations to solve problems

GRADE SEVEN GOALS

Variables and Patterns (Algebra)

- Recognize problem situations in which two or more quantitative variables are related to each other

- Identify quantitative variables in situations

- Describe patterns of change between two variables that are shown in words, tables and graphs of data

- Construct tables and graphs to display relations among variables

- Observe relationships between two variables as shown in a table, graph, or equation and describe how the relationship can be seen in each of the other forms of representation

- Use algebraic symbols to write equations relating variables

- Use tables, graphs, and equations to solve problems

- Use graphing calculators to construct tables and graphs of relations between variables and to answer questions about these relations

Stretching and Shrinking (Geometry)

- Identify similar figures by comparing corresponding parts

- Use scale factors and ratios to describe relationships among the side lengths of similar figures

- Construct similar polygons

- Draw shapes on coordinate grids and then use coordinate rules to stretch and shrink those shapes

- Predict the ways that stretching or shrinking a figure affect lengths, angle measures, perimeters, and areas

- Use the properties of similarity to calculate distances and heights that can't be directly measured

Comparing and Scaling (Number)

- Analyze comparison statements made about quantitative data
- Use ratios, fractions, differences, and percents to form comparison statements in a given situation, such as

  "What is the ratio of boys to girls in our class?"

  "What fraction of the class is going to the spring picnic?"

  "What percent of the girls play basketball?"

  "Which model of car has the best fuel economy?"

  "Which long-distance telephone company is more popular?"

- Judge whether comparison statements make sense and are useful
- See how forms of comparison statements are related, for example, a percent and a fraction comparison
- Make judgments about which statements are most informative or best reflect a particular point of view
- Decide when the most informative comparison is to find the difference between two quantities and when it is to form ratios between pairs of quantities
- Scale a ratio, rate, or fraction up or down to make a larger or smaller object or population with the same relative characteristics as the original
- Represent related data in tables
- Look for patterns in tables that will allow predictions to be made beyond the tables
- Write an equation to represent the pattern in a table of related variables
- Apply proportional reasoning to solve for the unknown part when one part of two equal ratios is unknown
- Set up and solve proportions that arise in applications
- Recognize that constant growth in a table is related to proportional situations
- Connect unit rates with the equation describing a situation

Accentuate the Negative (Number)

- Use appropriate notation to indicate positive and negative numbers
- Locate rational numbers (positive and negative fractions and decimals and zero) on a number line
- Compare and order rational numbers
- Understand the relationship between a positive or negative number and its opposite (additive inverse)
- Develop algorithms for adding, subtracting, multiplying, and dividing positive and negative numbers and write mathematics sentences to show relationships
- Write and use related fact families for addition/subtraction and multiplication/division to solve simple equations with missing facts
- Use parentheses and order of operations to make computational sequences clear
- Understand and use the Commutative Property for addition and multiplication of negative and positive numbers
- Apply the Distributive Property with positive and negative numbers to simplify expressions and solve problems
- Use positive and negative numbers to graph in four quadrants, model and answer questions about applied settings

Moving Straight Ahead (Algebra)

- Recognize problem situations in which two or more variables have a linear relationship to each other
- Construct tables, graphs, and symbolic equations that express linear relationships
- Translate information about linear relations given in a table, a graph, or an equation to one of the other forms
- Understand the connections between linear equations and patterns in the tables and graphs of those relations—rate of change, slope, and *y*-intercept
- Solve linear equations
- Solve problems and make decisions about linear relationships using information given in tables, graphs, and symbolic expressions
- Use tables, graphs, and equations of linear relations to answer interesting questions

Filling and Wrapping (Geometry)

- Understand volume as a measure of filling an object and surface area as a measure of wrapping or covering an object

- Use flat patterns to visualize and calculate surface areas of prisms and cylinders

- Develop formulas for the volumes of prisms, cylinders, cones, pyramids, and spheres either directly or by comparison with known volumes

- Understand that three-dimensional figures may have the same volume but quite different shapes and surface areas or that they may have the same surface area but different shapes and volumes

- Use surface area and volume to solve a variety of real-world problems

- Understand how changes in one or more dimensions of a rectangular prism or cylinder affects the prism's volume

- Extend students' understanding of similarity and scale factors to three-dimensional figures

- Understand the effect on surface area and volume of applying a scale factor to a rectangular prism

Data Distributions (Data Analysis)

- Apply the process of statistical investigation to pose questions, identify ways data are collected, determine strategies for analyzing data and interpreting the analysis in order to answer the questions posed

- Compare the distributions of data using their related centers, variability, and shapes

- Use the shape of a distribution to estimate the mean and median

- Recognize that variability occurs whenever data are collected and use properties of distributions to describe the variability in a given data set

- Identify sources of variability, including natural variability and variability that results from errors in measurement

- Decide if a difference among data values and/or summary measures matters

- Understand and decide when to use the mean and median to describe a distribution

- Make effective use of a variety of representations to display distributions, including tables, value bar graphs, dot or line plots, and bar graphs

- Understand and use counts or percents to report frequencies of occurrence of data

- Develop and use strategies for comparing equal-size and unequal-size data sets to solve problems

What Do You Expect? (Probability)

- Interpret experimental and theoretical probabilities and the relationship between them

- Distinguish between equally likely and non-equally likely outcomes

- Review strategies for identifying possible outcomes and analyzing probabilities, such as using lists or counting trees

- Understand that fairness implies equally likely outcomes

- Analyze situations that involve two-stages (or two actions)

- Use area models to analyze situations that involve two stages

- Determine the expected value of a probability situation

- Analyze binomial situations

- Use probability and expected value to make decisions

Numbers Around Us (Number)
Available in first edition ©2004.

- Choose sensible units for measuring

- Understand that a measurement has two components, a unit of measure and a count

- Build a repertoire of benchmarks to relate the measures of unfamiliar objects or events to the measures of objects or events that are personally meaningful

- Review the concept of place value as it relates to reading, writing, and using large numbers

- Read, write, and interpret the large numbers that occur in real-life measurements using standard, scientific, and calculator notation

- Review and extend the use of exponents

- Use estimates and rounded values for describing and comparing objects and events

- Develop strategies for operating with large numbers

- Choose sensible ways of comparing counts and measurements, including using differences, rates, and ratios

- Draw sensible conclusions from given information.

Thinking With Mathematical Models
(Algebra)

- Recognize linear and non-linear patterns in contexts, tables and graphs and describe those patterns using words and symbolic expressions
- Write equations to express linear patterns appearing in tables, graphs, and verbal contexts
- Write linear equations when specific information such as two points or a point and a slope, is given for a line
- Approximate linear data patterns with graph and equation models
- Solve linear equations
- Interpret inequalities
- Write equations describing inverse variation
- Use linear and inverse variation equations to solve problems and to make predictions and decisions

Looking For Pythagoras (Algebra)

- Relate the area of a square to the length of a side of the square
- Estimate square roots
- Develop strategies for finding the distance between two points on a coordinate grid
- Understand and apply the Pythagorean Theorem
- Use the Pythagorean Theorem to solve a variety of problems

Growing, Growing, Growing (Algebra)

- Recognize situations where one variable is an exponential function of another variable
- Recognize the connections between exponential equations and growth patterns in tables and graphs of those relations
- Construct equations to express exponential patterns that appear in data tables, graphs, and problem conditions
- Understand and apply the rules for operating on numerical expressions with exponents
- Solve problems about exponential growth and decay in a variety of situations such as science or business
- Compare exponential and linear relationships

Frogs, Fleas, and Painted Cubes
(Algebra)

- Recognize the patterns of change for quadratic relationships in a table, graph, equation, and problem situation
- Construct equations to express quadratic relationships that appear in tables, graphs and problem situations
- Recognize the connections between quadratic equations and patterns in tables and graphs of those relationships
- Use tables, graphs, and equations of quadratic relationships to locate maximum and minimum values of a dependent variable and the x- and y-intercepts and other important features of parabolas
- Recognize equivalent symbolic expressions for the dependent variable in quadratic relationships
- Use the distributive property to write equivalent quadratic expressions in factored form or expanded form
- Use tables, graphs, and equations of quadratic relations to solve problems in a variety of situations from geometry, science, and business
- Compare properties of quadratic, linear, and exponential relationships

Kaleidoscopes, Hubcaps, and Mirrors
(Geometry)

- Understand important properties of symmetry
- Recognize and describe symmetries of figures
- Use tools to examine symmetries and transformations
- Make figures with specified symmetries
- Identify basic design elements that can be used to replicate a given design
- Perform symmetry transformations of figures, including reflections, translations, and rotations
- Examine and describe the symmetries of a design made from a figure and its image(s) under a symmetry transformation
- Give precise mathematical directions for performing reflections, rotations, and translations
- Draw conclusions about a figure, such as measures of sides and angles, lengths of diagonals, or intersection points of diagonals, based on symmetries of the figure

- Understand that figures with the same shape and size are congruent
- Use symmetry transformations to explore whether two figures are congruent
- Give examples of minimum sets of measures of angles and sides that will guarantee that two triangles are congruent
- Use congruence of triangles to explore congruence of two quadrilaterals
- Use symmetry and congruence to deduce properties of figures
- Write coordinate rules for specifying the image of a general point (x, y) under particular transformations
- Use transformational geometry to describe motions, patterns, designs, and properties of shapes in the real world

Say It With Symbols (Algebra)

- Model situations with symbolic statements
- Write equivalent expressions
- Determine if different symbolic expressions are mathematically equivalent
- Interpret the information equivalent expressions represent in a given context
- Determine which equivalent expression to use to answer particular questions;
- Solve linear equations involving parentheses
- Solve quadratic equations by factoring
- Use equations to make predictions and decisions
- Analyze equations to determine the patterns of change in the tables and graphs that the equation represents
- Understand how and when symbols should be used to display relationships, generalizations, and proofs

The Shapes of Algebra (Algebra)

- Write and use equations of circles
- Determine lines are parallel or perpendicular by looking at patterns in their graphs, coordinates, and equations
- Find coordinates of points that divide line segments in various ratios
- Write inequalities that satisfy given situations
- Find solutions to inequalities represented by a graph or an equation

- Solve systems of linear equations by graphing, combining equations, and by substitution
- Write linear inequalities in two variables to match constraints in problem conditions
- Graph linear inequalities and systems of inequalities and use the results to solve problems

Samples and Populations
(Data Analysis)

- Revisit and use the process of statistical investigation to explore problems
- Distinguish between samples and populations and use information drawn from samples to draw conclusions about populations
- Explore the influence of sample size and of random or nonrandom sample selection
- Apply concepts from probability to select random samples from populations
- Compare sample distributions using measures of center (mean or median), measures of dispersion (range or percentiles), and data displays that group data (histograms and box-and-whisker plots)
- Explore relationships between paired values of numerical attributes

Clever Counting (Number)
Available in first edition ©2004.

- Recognize situations in which counting techniques apply
- Construct organized lists of outcomes for complex processes and uncover patterns that help in counting the outcomes of those processes
- Use diagrams, tables, and symbolic expressions to organize examples in listing and counting tasks
- Analyze the usefulness of counting trees and use counting trees
- Use mental arithmetic to make estimates in multiplication and division calculations
- Invent strategies for solving problems that involve counting
- Analyze counting problems involving choices in various contexts
- Differentiate among situations in which order does and does not matter and in which repeats are and are not allowed

- Analyze the number of paths through a network
- Compare the structures of networks with problems involving combinations
- Create networks that satisfy given constraints
- Apply thinking and reasoning skills to an open-ended situation in which assumptions must be made and create a persuasive argument to support a conjecture

Mathematics Process Goals

In setting mathematical goals for a school curriculum, the choice of content topics must be accompanied by an analysis of the kinds of thinking students will be able to demonstrate upon completion of the curriculum. The text below describes the eleven key mathematical processes developed in all the main content strands of *Connected Mathematics*.

Counting

Determining the number of elements in finite data sets, trees, graphs, or combinations by application of mental computation, estimation, counting principles, calculators and computers, and formal algorithms.

Visualizing

Recognizing and describing shape, size, and position of one-, two-, and three-dimensional objects and their images under transformations; interpreting graphical representations of data, functions, relations, and symbolic expressions.

Comparing

Describing relationships among quantities and shapes using concepts such as equality and inequality, order of magnitude, proportion, congruence, similarity, parallelism, perpendicularity, symmetry, and rates of growth or change.

Estimating

Determining reasonableness of answers. Using "benchmarks" to estimate measures. Using various strategies to approximate a calculation and to compare estimates.

Measuring

Assigning numbers as measures of geometric objects and probabilities of events. Choosing appropriate measures in a decision-making problem. Choosing appropriate units or scales and making approximate measurements or applying formal rules to find measures.

Modeling

Constructing, making inferences from, and interpreting concrete, symbolic, graphic, verbal, and algorithmic models of quantitative, visual, statistical, probabilistic, and algebraic relationships in problem situations. Translating information from one model to another.

Reasoning

Bringing to any problem situation the disposition and ability to observe, experiment, analyze, abstract, induce, deduce, extend, generalize, relate, and manipulate in order to find solutions or prove conjectures involving interesting and important patterns.

Connecting

Identifying ways in which problems, situations, and mathematical ideas are interrelated and applying knowledge gained in solving one problem to other problems.

Representing

Moving flexibly among graphic, numeric, symbolic, and verbal representations and recognizing the importance of having various representations of information in a situation.

Using Tools

Selecting and intelligently using calculators, computers, drawing tools, and physical models to represent, simulate, and manipulate patterns and relationships in problem settings.

Becoming Mathematicians

Having the disposition and imagination to inquire, investigate, tinker, dream, conjecture, invent, and communicate with others about mathematical ideas.

Alignment with the NCTM Principles and Standards 2000

In 1989, the National Council of Teachers of Mathematics (NCTM) released its *Curriculum and Evaluation Standards for School Mathematics*. This document provided guidance for developing and implementing a vision of mathematics and instruction that serves all students. In 2000, NCTM expanded and elaborated on the 1989 standards to create the *Principles and Standards for School Mathematics*. This document reflects the research on teaching, learning, and technology that has evolved over the past ten years. These standards have served as a guide in developing *Connected Mathematics*.

The following chart shows the alignment of *Connected Mathematics* with NCTM *Principles and Standards 2000*.

CONTENT STANDARDS

Number and Operations

Prime Time (Grade 6)

Bits and Pieces I (Grade 6)

Bits and Pieces II (Grade 6)

Bits and Pieces III (Grade 6)

Comparing and Scaling (Grade 7)

Accentuate the Negative (Grade 7)

Looking for Pythagoras (Grade 8)

Algebra

Variables and Patterns (Grade 7)

Moving Straight Ahead (Grade 7)

Thinking With Mathematical Models (Grade 8)

Looking for Pythagoras (Grade 8)

Growing, Growing, Growing (Grade 8)

Frogs, Fleas, and Painted Cubes (Grade 8)

Say It With Symbols (Grade 8)

Shapes of Algebra (Grade 8)

Geometry

Shapes and Designs (Grade 6)

Ruins of Montarek (Grade 6)

Stretching and Shrinking (Grade 7)

Filling and Wrapping (Grade 7)

Looking for Pythagoras (Grade 8)

Kaleidoscopes, Hubcaps, and Mirrors (Grade 8)

Measurement

Shapes and Designs (Grade 6)

Covering and Surrounding (Grade 6)

Stretching and Shrinking (Grade 7)

Filling and Wrapping (Grade 7)

Data Around Us (Grade 7)

Looking for Pythagoras (Grade 8)

Data Analysis and Probability

Data About Us (Grade 6)

How Likely Is It? (Grade 6)

What Do You Expect? (Grade 7)

Data Distributions (Grade 7)

Samples and Populations (Grade 8)

PROCESS STANDARDS

Problem Solving

All units
Because *Connected Mathematics* is a problem-centered curriculum, problem solving is an important part of every unit.

Reasoning and Proof

All units
Throughout the curriculum, students are encouraged to look for patterns, make conjectures, provide evidence for their conjectures, refine their conjectures and strategies, connect their knowledge, and extend their findings. Informal reasoning evolves into more deductive arguments as students proceed from Grade 6 through Grade 8.

Communication

All units

As students work on the problems, they must communicate ideas with others. Emphasis is placed on students' discussing problems in class, talking through their solutions, formalizing their conjectures and strategies, and learning to communicate their ideas to a more general audience. Students learn to express their ideas, solutions, and strategies using written explanations, graphs, tables, and equations.

Connections

All units

In all units, the mathematical content is connected to other units, to other areas of mathematics, to other school subjects, and to applications in the real world. Connecting and building on prior knowledge is important for building and retaining new knowledge.

Representation

All units

Throughout the units, students organize, record, and communicate information and ideas using words, pictures, graphs, tables, and symbols. They learn to choose appropriate representations for given situations and to translate among representations. Students also learn to interpret information presented in various forms.

Alignment with State Frameworks

Connected Mathematics addresses all content topics that might be required at middle school level. Because topics are covered in depth in individual units, districts may choose to use a particular unit at a grade level above or below its position in the teaching sequence. The chart on page 18 shows the recommended teaching order within each mathematics strand. If units are moved out of sequence to be taught *before* the recommended location and grade level, the district should carefully check to see that requisite connected units have been taught. Obvious examples are Bits and Pieces I, II, and III. These should not be taught in a different order. Another is the sequence of units in grade 7, Variables and Patterns, Stretching and Shrinking, Comparing and Scaling, Accentuate the Negative, and Moving Straight Ahead. These build on each other and should be taught in the recommended order.

Scope and Sequence for CMP2

Deep understanding of the concepts and skills are developed in the units listed. In some cases, the topics are introduced in one unit and more fully developed in a later unit. In other cases, the topics are revisited in the same or other units in Connections questions, or are used to develop understanding of new concepts. The development of a concept includes understanding relationships among and between concepts, as well as developing skills, procedures, and algorithms.

As a problem solving curriculum, every unit helps students develop a variety of strategies for solving problems, such as building models, making lists and tables, drawing diagrams, and solving simpler problems.

Key: I = introduced   M = mastered   R = reinforced; applied

Number and Operations			
	Grade 6	**Grade 7**	**Grade 8**
Whole Numbers			
divisors, factors, greatest common factor	*Prime Time* IM *Bits and Pieces I* R *Shapes and Designs* R *Covering and Surrounding* R *Data About Us* R	*Variables and Patterns* R *Comparing and Scaling* R *Accentuate the Negative* R *Filling and Wrapping* R	*Thinking With Mathematical Models* R *Growing, Growing, Growing* R *Frogs, Fleas, and Painted Cubes* R *Say It with Symbols* R
divisibility rules	*Prime Time* IM		*Growing, Growing, Growing* R *Say It with Symbols* R
multiples, least common multiple	*Prime Time* IM *Bits and Pieces I* R *Bits and Pieces II* R *Bits and Pieces III* R *Data About Us* R	*Comparing and Scaling* R	
even, odd numbers	*Prime Time* IM	*Variables and Patterns* R	*Say It With Symbols* R
prime numbers	*Prime Time* IM	*Filling and Wrapping* R	*Growing, Growing, Growing* R *Say It with Symbols* R
composite numbers	*Prime Time* IM		
squares	*Prime Time* IM *Shapes and Designs* R *Covering and Surrounding* R	*Stretching and Shrinking* R	*Looking for Pythagoras* R *Frogs, Fleas, and Painted Cubes* R *Say It with Symbols* R
square roots	*Prime Time* I	*Stretching and Shrinking* I	*Looking for Pythagoras* IM
prime factorization	*Prime Time* IM *Shapes and Designs* R		*Growing, Growing, Growing* R
place value	*Prime Time* R *Bits and Pieces I* R	*Data Around Us* R *Data Distributions* R	

Number and Operations (cont.)			
	Grade 6	**Grade 7**	**Grade 8**
Decimals			
place value	*Bits and Pieces I* IM *Bits and Pieces III* R	*Data Distributions* R	*Looking for Pythagoras* R *Growing, Growing, Growing* R
models (including grids and number lines)	*Bits and Pieces I* IM *Bits and Pieces II* R *Bits and Pieces III* R *Data About Us* R	*Variables and Patterns* R *Comparing and Scaling* R *What Do You Expect?* R *Data Distributions* R	*Thinking With Mathematical Models* R *Looking for Pythagoras* R *The Shapes of Algebra* R
comparing and ordering	*Bits and Pieces I* IM *Bits and Pieces II* R *Covering and Surrounding* R *Bits and Pieces III* R *How Likely Is It?* R	*Variables and Patterns* R *Comparing and Scaling* R *Accentuate the Negative* R *What Do You Expect?* R *Data Distributions* R	*Thinking With Mathematical Models* R *Looking for Pythagoras* R *Growing, Growing, Growing* R *The Shapes of Algebra* R *Samples and Populations* R
related to fractions and percents	*Bits and Pieces I* IM *Bits and Pieces II* R *Bits and Pieces III* R *How Likely Is It?* R *Data About Us* R	*Stretching and Shrinking* R *Comparing and Scaling* R *Filling and Wrapping* R *Data Distributions* R	*Thinking With Mathematical Models* R *Looking for Pythagoras* R *Growing, Growing, Growing* R
terminating and repeating decimals	*Bits and Pieces III* IM		*Looking for Pythagoras* R
estimating/benchmarks	*Bits and Pieces I* IM *Bits and Pieces II* R *Bits and Pieces III* R	*Comparing and Scaling* R *Filling and Wrapping* R *Data Distributions* R	*Looking for Pythagoras* R
rounding	*Bits and Pieces I* IM *Bits and Pieces III* R *How Likely Is It?* R	*Filling and Wrapping* R *Data Distributions* R	*Looking for Pythagoras* R *Growing, Growing, Growing* R
scientific notation		see also *Data Around Us* ©2004 IM	*Growing, Growing, Growing* IM
operations with	*Bits and Pieces III* IM *How Likely Is It?* R *Data About Us* R	*Stretching and Shrinking* R *Comparing and Scaling* R *Accentuate the Negative* R *Moving Straight Ahead* R *Filling and Wrapping* R *What Do You Expect?* R *Data Distributions* R	*Thinking With Mathematical Models* R *Looking for Pythagoras* R *Growing, Growing, Growing* R *Samples and Populations* R
Fractions			
comparing and ordering	*Bits and Pieces I* IM *Shapes and Designs* R *Bits and Pieces II* R *Covering and Surrounding* R *Bits and Pieces III* R *How Likely Is It?* R	*Variables and Patterns* R *Comparing and Scaling* R *Accentuate the Negative* R *What Do You Expect?* R *Data Distributions* R	*Thinking With Mathematical Models* R *Looking for Pythagoras* R *Growing, Growing, Growing* R *The Shapes of Algebra* R *Samples and Populations* R

Number and Operations (cont.)			
	Grade 6	**Grade 7**	**Grade 8**

related to decimals and percents	*Bits and Pieces I* IM
	Bits and Pieces II R
	Bits and Pieces III R
	How Likely Is It? R
	Data About Us R
		Stretching and Shrinking R
		Comparing and Scaling R
		What Do You Expect? R
		Data Distributions R
			*Thinking With
			  Mathematical Models* R
			Looking for Pythagoras R
			*Growing, Growing,
			  Growing* R

equivalent	*Bits and Pieces I* IM *Shapes and Designs* R *Bits and Pieces II* R *Bits and Pieces III* R *How Likely Is It?* R	*Stretching and Shrinking* R *Comparing and Scaling* R *Moving Straight Ahead* R *What Do You Expect?* R	*Growing, Growing, Growing* R *Samples and Populations* R
estimating/benchmarks	*Bits and Pieces I* IM *Bits and Pieces II* R *Bits and Pieces III* R *How Likely Is It?* R	*Comparing and Scaling* R *What Do You Expect?* R *Data Distributions* R	*Samples and Populations* R
models	*Bits and Pieces I* IM *Shapes and Designs* R *Bits and Pieces II* R *Bits and Pieces III* R *How Likely Is It?* R	*Comparing and Scaling* R *Filling and Wrapping* R *What Do You Expect?* R	*Looking for Pythagoras* R
reciprocals	*Bits and Pieces II* IM	*Moving Straight Ahead* R	*Thinking With Mathematical Models* R

operations with	*Bits and Pieces I* I
	Shapes and Designs I
	Bits and Pieces II IM
	*Covering and
	  Surrounding* R
	Bits and Pieces III R
	How Likely Is It? R
	Data About Us R
		Variables and Patterns R
		Stretching and Shrinking R
		Accentuate the Negative R
		Moving Straight Ahead R
		Filling and Wrapping R
		What Do You Expect? R
		Data Distributions R
			*Thinking With
			  Mathematical Models* R
			Looking for Pythagoras R
			*Growing, Growing,
			  Growing* R
			Say It with Symbols R

Ratio and Proportion			

ratios, rates, unit rates	*Bits and Pieces I* I
	Shapes and Designs I
	Bits and Pieces II I
	Bits and Pieces III I
	How Likely Is It? I
	Data About Us I
		Variables and Patterns I
		Stretching and Shrinking I
		Comparing and Scaling IM
		Moving Straight Ahead R
		Filling and Wrapping R
		Data Distributions R
			*Thinking With
			  Mathematical Models* R
			Looking for Pythagoras R
			*Growing, Growing,
			  Growing* R
			*Frogs, Fleas, and Painted
			  Cubes* R
			The Shapes of Algebra R
			Samples and Populations R

equivalent ratios	*Bits and Pieces I* I
	Shapes and Designs I
	Bits and Pieces II I
	Bits and Pieces III I
	How Likely Is It? I
		Stretching and Shrinking IM
		Comparing and Scaling R
		Moving Straight Ahead R
		What Do You Expect? R
		Data Distributions R
			*Thinking With
			  Mathematical Models* R
			Looking for Pythagoras R
			*Growing, Growing,
			  Growing* R
			Samples and Populations R

Number and Operations (cont.)			
	Grade 6	**Grade 7**	**Grade 8**
proportions	*Bits and Pieces I* I *Bits and Pieces II* I *Bits and Pieces III* I *How Likely Is It?* I	*Stretching and Shrinking* I *Comparing and Scaling* IM *Moving Straight Ahead* R	*Thinking With* *Mathematical Models* R
comparing proportional and nonproportional relationships	*Bits and Pieces I* I *Bits and Pieces III* I *How Likely Is It?* I *Data About Us* I	*Variables and Patterns* I *Stretching and Shrinking* I *Comparing and Scaling* IM *Moving Straight Ahead* R *What Do You Expect?* R *Data Distributions* R	*Thinking With* *Mathematical Models* R

scaling/scale factors	*Bits and Pieces I* I
	Bits and Pieces III I
	How Likely Is It? I
		Stretching and Shrinking IM
		Comparing and Scaling R
		What Do You Expect? R
			Thinking With
			  Mathematical Models R
			Looking for Pythagoras R
			Growing, Growing,
			  Growing R
			Frogs, Fleas, and Painted
			  Cubes R
			Kaleidoscopes, Hubcaps,
			  and Mirrors R
			Say It with Symbols R
			The Shapes of Algebra R

scale factors with similar 3-dimensional figures		*Filling and Wrapping* IM	
estimating	*Bits and Pieces I* I *Bits and Pieces III* I *How Likely Is It?* I *Data About Us* I	*Stretching and Shrinking* I *Comparing and Scaling* IM *Filling and Wrapping* R *What Do You Expect?* R *Data Distributions* R	*Thinking With* *Mathematical Models* R

proportional reasoning	*Bits and Pieces I* I
	Bits and Pieces II I
	Bits and Pieces III I
	How Likely Is It? I
		Variables and Patterns I
		Stretching and Shrinking I
		Comparing and Scaling IM
		Moving Straight Ahead R
		Filling and Wrapping R
		What Do You Expect? R
		Data Distributions R
			Thinking With
			  Mathematical Models R
			Looking for Pythagoras R
			Growing, Growing,
			  Growing R
			Kaleidoscopes, Hubcaps,
			  and Mirrors R
			Say It with Symbols R
			The Shapes of Algebra R
			Samples and Populations R

Percents			

related to fractions and decimals	*Bits and Pieces I* IM
	Bits and Pieces II R
	Bits and Pieces III R
	How Likely Is It? R
	Data About Us R
		Stretching and Shrinking R
		Comparing and Scaling R
		What Do You Expect? R
		Data Distributions R
			Thinking With
			  Mathematical Models R
			Growing, Growing,
			  Growing R
			Say It with Symbols R
			Samples and Populations R

models	*Bits and Pieces I* IM *Bits and Pieces III* R *How Likely Is It?* R	*Stretching and Shrinking* R *Comparing and Scaling* R *What Do You Expect?* R	*Samples and Populations* R

Number and Operations (cont.)			
	Grade 6	**Grade 7**	**Grade 8**
estimating/benchmarks	*Bits and Pieces I* IM *Bits and Pieces II* R *Bits and Pieces III* R *How Likely Is It?* R *Data About Us* R	*What Do You Expect?* R *Data Distributions* R	*Samples and Populations* R
finding (and solving x% of y = z)	*Bits and Pieces I* I *Bits and Pieces III* IM *How Likely Is It?* R *Data About Us* R	*Variables and Patterns* R *Stretching and Shrinking* R *Comparing and Scaling* R *Moving Straight Ahead* R *What Do You Expect?* R *Data Distributions* R	*Growing, Growing, Growing* R *The Shapes of Algebra* R *Samples and Populations* R
percent of a number	*Bits and Pieces I* I *Bits and Pieces III* IM *How Likely Is It?* R *Data About Us* R	*Stretching and Shrinking* R *Comparing and Scaling* R *Moving Straight Ahead* R *What Do You Expect?* R *Data Distributions* R	*Growing, Growing, Growing* R *Say It with Symbols* R *Samples and Populations* R
solving problems with	*Bits and Pieces III* IM *How Likely Is It?* R	*Stretching and Shrinking* R *Comparing and Scaling* R *What Do You Expect?* R *Data Distributions* R	*Growing, Growing, Growing* R *Say It with Symbols* R *Samples and Populations* R
Integers			
models	*Bits and Pieces II* I	*Accentuate the Negative* IM *Data Distributions* R	*The Shapes of Algebra* R
opposites/inverse operations		*Accentuate the Negative* IM *Moving Straight Ahead* R	*Thinking With Mathematical Models* R *Looking for Pythagoras* R *Say It with Symbols* R *The Shapes of Algebra* R
absolute value		*Accentuate the Negative* IM	
comparing and ordering		*Accentuate the Negative* IM *Data Distributions* R	*Thinking With Mathematical Models* R *The Shapes of Algebra* R
on a number line	*Bits and Pieces II* I	*Accentuate the Negative* IM *What Do You Expect?* R	*Thinking With Mathematical Models* R *The Shapes of Algebra* R
operations with		*Accentuate the Negative* IM *Moving Straight Ahead* R *What Do You Expect?* R	*Thinking With Mathematical Models* R *Frogs, Fleas, and Painted Cubes* R *Say It with Symbols* R *The Shapes of Algebra* R
solving problems with	*Bits and Pieces II* I	*Accentuate the Negative* IM	*Say It with Symbols* R

Number and Operations (cont.)			
	Grade 6	**Grade 7**	**Grade 8**
Irrational Numbers			
models	*Covering and Surrounding* I *How Likely Is It?* I	*Filling and Wrapping* I	*Looking for Pythagoras* IM
pi	*Covering and Surrounding* IM *Bits and Pieces III* R *How Likely Is It?* R	*Variables and Patterns* R *Filling and Wrapping* R	*Looking for Pythagoras* R
Pythagorean Theorem			*Looking for Pythagoras* IM *Kaleidoscopes, Hubcaps, and Mirrors* R *The Shapes of Algebra* R
square roots	*How Likely Is It?* I		*Looking for Pythagoras* IM *The Shapes of Algebra* R
estimating			*Looking for Pythagoras* IM *The Shapes of Algebra* R
Real Numbers	*Prime Time* I		
defined			*Looking for Pythagoras* IM
Order of Operations		*Accentuate the Negative* IM *Moving Straight Ahead* R	*Thinking With Mathematical Models* R *Frogs, Fleas, and Painted Cubes* R *Say It with Symbols* R
exponential form (notation)	*Prime Time* IM *Bits and Pieces III* R	*Variables and Patterns* R *Stretching and Shrinking* R *Accentuate the Negative* R	*Growing, Growing, Growing* R *Say It with Symbols* R *The Shapes of Algebra* R
laws of exponents			*Growing, Growing, Growing* IM *Say It with Symbols* R
Properties			
distributive	*Bits and Pieces II* I *Covering and Surrounding* I *Bits and Pieces III* I	*Accentuate the Negative* IM *Moving Straight Ahead* R	*Frogs, Fleas, and Painted Cubes* R *Say It with Symbols* R *The Shapes of Algebra* R
commutative	*Prime Time* I	*Accentuate the Negative* IM *Moving Straight Ahead* R	*Say It with Symbols* R
associative		*Accentuate the Negative* I	*Say It with Symbols* IM

Data Analysis and Probability			
	Grade 6	**Grade 7**	**Grade 8**
Data Investigation			
Note: Opportunities for students to question, collect, analyze, and interpret data occur in almost every unit.			
collecting data	*How Likely Is It?* I *Data About Us* IM	*Variables and Patterns* R *Moving Straight Ahead* R *Filling and Wrapping* R *What Do You Expect?* R *Data Distributions* R	*Thinking with Mathematical Models* R *Looking for Pythagoras* R *Growing, Growing, Growing* R *Samples and Populations* R
analyze data	*Bits and Pieces III* I *How Likely Is It?* I *Data About Us* IM	*Variables and Patterns* R *Comparing and Scaling* R *Moving Straight Ahead* R *Filling and Wrapping* R *What Do You Expect?* R *Data Distributions* R	*Thinking with Mathematical Models* R *Looking for Pythagoras* R *Growing, Growing, Growing* R *Samples and Populations* R
interpret data	*Bits and Pieces III* I *How Likely Is It?* I *Data About Us* IM	*Variables and Patterns* R *Comparing and Scaling* R *Moving Straight Ahead* R *Filling and Wrapping* R *What Do You Expect?* R *Data Distributions* R	*Thinking with Mathematical Models* R *Looking for Pythagoras* R *Growing, Growing, Growing* R *Samples and Populations* R
samples	*How Likely Is It?* I *Data About Us* I	*What Do You Expect?* I	*Samples and Populations* IM
randomness	*How Likely Is It?* IM	*What Do You Expect?* R	*Samples and Populations* R
draw conclusions/make predictions	*How Likely Is It?* I *Data About Us* IM	*What Do You Expect?* R *Comparing and Scaling* R *Moving Straight Ahead* R *Filling and Wrapping* R *Data Distributions* R	*Thinking with Mathematical Models* R *Looking for Pythagoras* R *Growing, Growing, Growing* R *Samples and Populations* R
compare data	*How Likely Is It?* I *Data About Us* I	*Variables and Patterns* I *Comparing and Scaling* I *Moving Straight Ahead* I *Filling and Wrapping* R *What Do You Expect?* I *Data Distributions* IM	*Thinking with Mathematical Models* R *Samples and Populations* R
conduct surveys	*How Likely Is It?* I *Data About Us* I	*Data Distributions* I	*Samples and Populations* R
evaluate methods of sampling	*How Likely Is It?* I *Data About Us* I	*What Do You Expect?* I *Data Distributions* I	*Samples and Populations* IM
Data Representation			
Note: Opportunities for students to read, create, or use tables occur in almost every unit.			
line plots	*How Likely Is It?* I *Data About Us* IM	*Variables and Patterns* R *What Do You Expect?* R *Data Distributions* R	*Samples and Populations* R

MATHEMATICS CONTENT

Data Analysis and Probability (cont.)			
	Grade 6	**Grade 7**	**Grade 8**
single, double, stacked bar graphs	*Bits and Pieces I* I *Bits and Pieces III* I *How Likely Is It?* I *Data About Us* IM	*Comparing and Scaling* R *Data Distributions* R	*Growing, Growing,* *Growing* R *The Shapes of Algebra* R *Samples and Populations* R
stem-and-leaf plots	*Data About Us* IM	*Data Distributions* R	*Samples and Populations* R

coordinate graphs	*Covering and*
	  Surrounding I
	Data About Us I
		Variables and Patterns IM
		Comparing and Scaling R
		Accentuate the Negative R
		Moving Straight Ahead R
		Filling and Wrapping R
		Data Distributions R
			Thinking with
			  Mathematical Models R
			Looking for Pythagoras R
			Growing, Growing,
			  Growing R
			Frogs, Fleas, and Painted
			  Cubes R
			Kaleidoscopes, Hubcaps,
			  and Mirrors R
			Say It With Symbols R
			The Shapes of Algebra R
			Samples and Populations R

tables	*Shapes and Designs* R
	Covering and
	  Surrounding I
	Data About Us IM
		Variables and Patterns IM
		Comparing and Scaling R
		Moving Straight Ahead R
		Filling and Wrapping R
		Data Distributions R
			Thinking with
			  Mathematical Models R
			Looking for Pythagoras R
			Growing, Growing,
			  Growing R
			Frogs, Fleas, and Painted
			  Cubes R
			Say It With Symbols R
			Samples and Populations R

frequency tables	*Data About Us* IM *How Likely Is It?* R	*Comparing and Scaling* R *Data Distributions* R	
circle graphs (pie charts)	*Bits and Pieces III* IM *Data About Us* R	*Data Distributions* R	*The Shapes of Algebra* R *Samples and Populations* R
histograms			*Samples and* *Populations* IM
box-and-whisker plots (box plots)			*Samples and* *Populations* IM
scatter plots	*Data About Us* I	*Variables and Patterns* I *Data Distributions* IM	*Thinking with* *Mathematical Models* R *Samples and Populations* R
analyze trends/trend lines	*Data About Us* I	*Variables and Patterns* I *Comparing and Scaling* I *Moving Straight Ahead* I *Data Distributions* I	*Thinking with* *Mathematical Models* IM *Samples and Populations* R
decide on appropriateness and effectiveness	*Bits and Pieces III* I *How Likely Is It?* I *Data About Us* IM	*Comparing and Scaling* R *Data Distributions* R	*Samples and Populations* R

Data Analysis and Probability (cont.)

	Grade 6	Grade 7	Grade 8
Describing Data			
mode	*Data About Us* IM	*Data Distributions* R	*Samples and Populations* R
median	*Data About Us* IM	*Variables and Patterns* R *Accentuate the Negative* R *Data Distributions* R	*Samples and Populations* R
mean (average)	*Bits and Pieces III* I *Data About Us* IM	*Variables and Patterns* R *Accentuate the Negative* R *Data Distributions* R	*Thinking with Mathematical Models* IM *Samples and Populations* R
range	*Data About Us* IM	*Accentuate the Negative* R *Data Distributions* R	*Samples and Populations* R
outliers	*Data About Us* I	*Data Distributions* I	*Samples and Populations* IM
shape of data	*Data About Us* I	*Data Distributions* IM	*Samples and Populations* R
data distribution	*Data About Us* I	*Data Distributions* IM	*Samples and Populations* R
quartiles, interquartile range (IQR)			*Samples and Populations* IM
maximum, minimum	*Covering and Surrounding* I	*Data Distributions* IM	*Frogs, Fleas, and Painted Cubes* R *Samples and Populations* R
choose the best summary statistic and representation	*Data About Us* IM	*Data Distributions* R	*Samples and Populations* R
Probability			
predicting, computing	*How Likely Is It?* IM	*Variables and Patterns* R *Stretching and Shrinking* R *Comparing and Scaling* R *What Do You Expect?* R *Data Distributions* R	*Thinking With Mathematical Models* R *The Shapes of Algebra* R *Samples and Populations* R
equally and unequally likely outcomes	*How Likely Is It?* IM	*What Do You Expect?* R	*The Shapes of Algebra* R
certain, possible, impossible events	*How Likely Is It?* IM	*What Do You Expect?* R	
experimental	*How Likely Is It?* IM	*Variables and Patterns* R *Comparing and Scaling* R *What Do You Expect?* R	
theoretical	*How Likely Is It?* IM	*Stretching and Shrinking* R *Comparing and Scaling* R *What Do You Expect?* R	
dependent and independent events		*What Do You Expect?* IM	
expected value	*How Likely Is It?* I	*What Do You Expect?* IM	
fair and unfair games	*How Likely Is It?* IM	*What Do You Expect?* R	

MATHEMATICS CONTENT

Data Analysis and Probability (cont.)			
	Grade 6	**Grade 7**	**Grade 8**
lists, charts, tree diagrams, area models	*How Likely Is It?* I	*Variables and Patterns* I *Stretching and Shrinking* I *Comparing and Scaling* I *What Do You Expect?* IM	
counting techniques	*How Likely Is It?* I	*What Do You Expect?* IM	*Say It with Symbols* R see also *Clever Counting* ©2004 M
simulations/experiments	*How Likely Is It?* IM	*Variables and Patterns* R *Moving Straight Ahead* R *What Do You Expect?* R	*Thinking With* * Mathematical Models* R *Growing, Growing,* * Growing* R *Samples and Populations* R

Measurement			

Angles			
estimating	*Shapes and Designs* IM *Bits and Pieces III* R *How Likely Is It?* R	*Stretching and Shrinking* R *Comparing and Scaling* R *Data Distributions* R	*Looking for Pythagoras* R *Kaleidoscopes, Hubcaps,* * and Mirrors* R
measuring	*Shapes and Designs* IM *Bits and Pieces III* R *How Likely Is It?* R	*Stretching and Shrinking* R *Comparing and Scaling* R	*Looking for Pythagoras* R *Kaleidoscopes, Hubcaps,* * and Mirrors* R
of similar polygons	*Shapes and Designs* I	*Stretching and* * Shrinking* IM *Comparing and Scaling* R	*Looking for Pythagoras* R *Kaleidoscopes, Hubcaps,* * and Mirrors* R
triangle, special right			*Looking for Pythagoras* IM

Perimeter			
polygons	*Shapes and Designs* I *Covering and* * Surrounding* IM *Bits and Pieces III* R	*Variables and Patterns* R *Stretching and Shrinking* R *Moving Straight Ahead* R *Filling and Wrapping* R	*Thinking With* * Mathematical Models* R *Looking for Pythagoras* R *Frogs, Fleas, and Painted* * Cubes* R *Kaleidoscopes, Hubcaps,* * and Mirrors* R *Say It with Symbols* R *The Shapes of Algebra* R
circles (circumference)	*Covering and* * Surrounding* IM *Bits and Pieces III* R	*Variables and Patterns* R *Stretching and Shrinking* R *Moving Straight Ahead* R *Filling and Wrapping* R	*Growing, Growing,* * Growing* R *Frogs, Fleas, and Painted* * Cubes* R *Kaleidoscopes, Hubcaps,* * and Mirrors* R *Say It with Symbols* R *The Shapes of Algebra* R
irregular polygons	*Covering and* * Surrounding* IM *Bits and Pieces III* R	*Stretching and Shrinking* R *Filling and Wrapping* R	*Looking for Pythagoras* R *Kaleidoscopes, Hubcaps,* * and Mirrors* R *Say It with Symbols* R

Measurement (cont.)			
	Grade 6	**Grade 7**	**Grade 8**
constant perimeter, changing area	*Covering and Surrounding* IM	*Variables and Patterns* R *Moving Straight Ahead* R	*Thinking With Mathematical Models* R *Frogs, Fleas, and Painted Cubes* R *Say It with Symbols* R
relationships of sides and perimeters of similar figures		*Stretching and Shrinking* IM *Comparing and Scaling* R	*Thinking With Mathematical Models* R *Growing, Growing, Growing* R *Frogs, Fleas, and Painted Cubes* R *The Shapes of Algebra* R
Area			
rectangles	*Prime Time* I *Bits and Pieces I* I *Shapes and Designs* R *Bits and Pieces II* I *Covering and Surrounding* IM *Bits and Pieces III* R	*Variables and Patterns* R *Stretching and Shrinking* R *Comparing and Scaling* R *Moving Straight Ahead* R *Filling and Wrapping* R *What Do You Expect?* R	*Thinking With Mathematical Models* R *Looking for Pythagoras* R *Growing, Growing, Growing* R *Frogs, Fleas, and Painted Cubes* R *Kaleidoscopes, Hubcaps, and Mirrors* R *Say It with Symbols* R *The Shapes of Algebra* R
triangles	*Covering and Surrounding* IM *Bits and Pieces III* R	*Variables and Patterns* R *Stretching and Shrinking* R *Moving Straight Ahead* R *Filling and Wrapping* R	*Looking for Pythagoras* R *Growing, Growing, Growing* R *Frogs, Fleas, and Painted Cubes* R *Kaleidoscopes, Hubcaps, and Mirrors* R *Say It with Symbols* R
parallelograms	*Covering and Surrounding* IM *Bits and Pieces III* R	*Variables and Patterns* R *Stretching and Shrinking* R *Filling and Wrapping* R	*Frogs, Fleas, and Painted Cubes* R *Kaleidoscopes, Hubcaps, and Mirrors* R
circles	*Covering and Surrounding* IM *Bits and Pieces III* R	*Variables and Patterns* R *Stretching and Shrinking* R *Moving Straight Ahead* R *Filling and Wrapping* R	*Looking for Pythagoras* R *Growing, Growing, Growing* R *Frogs, Fleas, and Painted Cubes* R *Kaleidoscopes, Hubcaps, and Mirrors* R *Say It with Symbols* R *The Shapes of Algebra* R
irregular polygons	*Bits and Pieces I* I *Bits and Pieces II* I *Covering and Surrounding* IM *Bits and Pieces III* R	*Stretching and Shrinking* R *Filling and Wrapping* R	*Looking for Pythagoras* R *Kaleidoscopes, Hubcaps, and Mirrors* R *Say It with Symbols* R *The Shapes of Algebra* R

MATHEMATICS CONTENT

	Measurement (cont.)		
	Grade 6	**Grade 7**	**Grade 8**
trapezoids	*Covering and Surrounding* I		*Frogs, Fleas, and Painted Cubes* IM *Say It with Symbols* R
constant area, changing perimeter	*Covering and Surrounding* IM	*Variables and Patterns* R	*Thinking With Mathematical Models* R *Frogs, Fleas, and Painted Cubes* R
relationships of areas of similar figures		*Stretching and Shrinking* IM *Comparing and Scaling* R *Filling and Wrapping* R *What Do You Expect?* R	*Looking for Pythagoras* R *Growing, Growing, Growing* R *Frogs, Fleas, and Painted Cubes* R *Kaleidoscopes, Hubcaps, and Mirrors* R *The Shapes of Algebra* R
Volume			
models		*Filling and Wrapping* IM *What Do You Expect?* R	*Frogs, Fleas, and Painted Cubes* R
cubes		*Filling and Wrapping* IM *What Do You Expect?* R	*Looking for Pythagoras* R *Growing, Growing, Growing* R *Frogs, Fleas, and Painted Cubes* R
prisms		*Filling and Wrapping* IM *What Do You Expect?* R	*Thinking With Mathematical Models* R *Looking for Pythagoras* R *Frogs, Fleas, and Painted Cubes* R *Say It with Symbols* R
cylinders		*Filling and Wrapping* IM	*Looking for Pythagoras* R *Growing, Growing, Growing* R *Frogs, Fleas, and Painted Cubes* R *Kaleidoscopes, Hubcaps, and Mirrors* R *Say It with Symbols* R *The Shapes of Algebra* R
cones		*Filling and Wrapping* IM	*Thinking With Mathematical Models* R *Looking for Pythagoras* R *Say It with Symbols* R
pyramids		*Filling and Wrapping* IM	*Looking for Pythagoras* R *Say It with Symbols* R
spheres		*Filling and Wrapping* IM	*Say It with Symbols* R
irregular figures		*Filling and Wrapping* IM	*Say It with Symbols* R

	Grade 6	Grade 7	Grade 8
Measurement (cont.)			
similar figures and scale factors		*Filling and Wrapping* IM	
effects when the dimensions of a solid are changed proportionally		*Filling and Wrapping* IM	*Thinking With Mathematical Models* R *Growing, Growing, Growing* R *Frogs, Fleas, and Painted Cubes* R
Surface Area			
flat patterns (nets) for solid figures	*Covering and Surrounding* R *How Likely Is It?* R	*Filling and Wrapping* IM	*Thinking With Mathematical Models* R *Looking for Pythagoras* R *Frogs, Fleas, and Painted Cubes* R *Kaleidoscopes, Hubcaps, and Mirrors* R *Say It with Symbols* R *The Shapes of Algebra* R
other models		*Filling and Wrapping* IM	*Thinking With Mathematical Models* R *Looking for Pythagoras* R
cubes		*Filling and Wrapping* IM	*Thinking With Mathematical Models* R *Frogs, Fleas, and Painted Cubes* R *Say It with Symbols* R
prisms		*Filling and Wrapping* IM	*Thinking With Mathematical Models* R *Looking for Pythagoras* R *Frogs, Fleas, and Painted Cubes* R *Say It with Symbols* R *The Shapes of Algebra* R
cylinders		*Filling and Wrapping* IM	*Thinking With Mathematical Models* R *Frogs, Fleas, and Painted Cubes* R *Say It with Symbols* R *The Shapes of Algebra* R
pyramids	*How Likely Is It?* I	*Filling and Wrapping* I	*Looking for Pythagoras* I
irregular figures			*Say It with Symbols* I
formulas		*Filling and Wrapping* IM	

Measurement (cont.)			
	Grade 6	**Grade 7**	**Grade 8**
Finding Missing Lengths			
similar figures using ratios or scale factor		*Stretching and Shrinking* IM *Comparing and Scaling* R *Moving Straight Ahead* R	*Thinking With Mathematical Models* R *Looking for Pythagoras* R *Kaleidoscopes, Hubcaps, and Mirrors* R
on a coordinate grid			*Looking for Pythagoras* IM *The Shapes of Algebra* R
using the Pythagorean Theorem			*Looking for Pythagoras* IM *Growing, Growing, Growing* R *Kaleidoscopes, Hubcaps, and Mirrors* R *Say It with Symbols* R *The Shapes of Algebra* R
Indirect			
similar triangles		*Stretching and Shrinking* IM *Comparing and Scaling* R	*Looking for Pythagoras* R *Kaleidoscopes, Hubcaps, and Mirrors* R
solving problems with		*Stretching and Shrinking* IM *Comparing and Scaling* R	*Looking for Pythagoras* R *Kaleidoscopes, Hubcaps, and Mirrors* R
Units of Measure			
converting within the same measurement system	*Shapes and Designs* R	*Moving Straight Ahead* R *Filling and Wrapping* R	
converting among customary and metric		*Comparing and Scaling* R *Moving Straight Ahead* R *Data About Us* R	
Geometry			
Line			
parallel lines	*Shapes and Designs* IM	*Stretching and Shrinking* R *Moving Straight Ahead* R	*Thinking With Mathematical Models* R *Looking for Pythagoras* R *The Shapes of Algebra* R
perpendicular lines	*Shapes and Designs* IM	*Moving Straight Ahead* R	*Looking for Pythagoras* R *Kaleidoscopes, Hubcaps, and Mirrors* R *The Shapes of Algebra* R
transversals	*Shapes and Designs* IM	*Stretching and Shrinking* R	*Kaleidoscopes, Hubcaps, and Mirrors* R
midpoints	*Shapes and Designs* IM	*Stretching and Shrinking* R	*Looking for Pythagoras* R *The Shapes of Algebra* R

	Grade 6	Grade 7	Grade 8
Geometry (cont.)			
Angles			
classifying	*Shapes and Designs* IM		
congruent	*Shapes and Designs* IM	*Stretching and Shrinking* R	*Looking for Pythagoras* R *Kaleidoscopes, Hubcaps, and Mirrors* R
complementary and supplementary		*Stretching and Shrinking* IM *Filling and Wrapping* R	
of a polygon	*Shapes and Designs* IM	*Variables and Patterns* R *Stretching and Shrinking* R	*Looking for Pythagoras* R *Kaleidoscopes, Hubcaps, and Mirrors* R
n-gon angle sum	*Shapes and Designs* IM *Bits and Pieces III* R	*Variables and Patterns* R *Moving Straight Ahead* R	*Kaleidoscopes, Hubcaps, and Mirrors* R *The Shapes of Algebra* R
on a circular grid	*Shapes and Designs* IM		
corresponding (parallel lines)	*Shapes and Designs* IM	*Stretching and Shrinking* R	*Kaleidoscopes, Hubcaps, and Mirrors* R
Polygons			
properties of	*Shapes and Designs* IM		*Looking for Pythagoras* R *Kaleidoscopes, Hubcaps, and Mirrors* R *The Shapes of Algebra* R
regular	*Shapes and Designs* IM	*Variables and Patterns* R *Moving Straight Ahead* R	
tilings/tessellations	*Shapes and Designs* IM	*Stretching and Shrinking* R	*Kaleidoscopes, Hubcaps, and Mirrors* R
diagonals	*Shapes and Designs* IM	*Variables and Patterns* R *Moving Straight Ahead* R	*Looking for Pythagoras* R *Growing, Growing, Growing* R *Frogs, Fleas, and Painted Cubes* R *Kaleidoscopes, Hubcaps, and Mirrors* R
triangles, classifying	*Shapes and Designs* IM	*Stretching and Shrinking* R *Moving Straight Ahead* R *Filling and Wrapping* R	*Looking for Pythagoras* R *Kaleidoscopes, Hubcaps, and Mirrors* R
quadrilaterals, classifying	*Shapes and Designs* IM	*Stretching and Shrinking* R *Moving Straight Ahead* R	*Looking for Pythagoras* R *Kaleidoscopes, Hubcaps, and Mirrors* R *The Shapes of Algebra* R

MATHEMATICS CONTENT

Geometry (cont.)			
	Grade 6	**Grade 7**	**Grade 8**
similar		*Stretching and Shrinking* IM *Moving Straight Ahead* R *Filling and Wrapping* R	*Looking for Pythagoras* R *Growing, Growing, Growing* R *Kaleidoscopes, Hubcaps, and Mirrors* R *The Shapes of Algebra* R
congruent	*Covering and Surrounding* I *How Likely Is It?* I	*Stretching and Shrinking* I	*Looking for Pythagoras* I *Kaleidoscopes, Hubcaps, and Mirrors* IM
enlarging and shrinking (dilations)		*Stretching and Shrinking* IM *Moving Straight Ahead* R	*Looking for Pythagoras* R *Growing, Growing, Growing* R *Kaleidoscopes, Hubcaps, and Mirrors* R *The Shapes of Algebra* R
drawing on coordinate grid		*Stretching and Shrinking* IM *Moving Straight Ahead* R	*Looking for Pythagoras* R *Kaleidoscopes, Hubcaps, and Mirrors* R *The Shapes of Algebra* R
Pythagorean Theorem			*Looking for Pythagoras* IM *Say It with Symbols* R *The Shapes of Algebra* R
Circles			
Relationship between radius/diameter/circumference	*Covering and Surrounding* IM	*Filling and Wrapping* R	*Looking for Pythagoras* R *Frogs, Fleas, and Painted Cubes* R *Kaleidoscopes, Hubcaps, and Mirrors* R *The Shapes of Algebra* R
Three-Dimensional Figures			
cubes		*Filling and Wrapping* IM	*Thinking With Mathematical Models* R *Looking for Pythagoras* R *Frogs, Fleas, and Painted Cubes* R
prisms		*Filling and Wrapping* IM	*Looking for Pythagoras* R
cylinders/spheres/cones		*Filling and Wrapping* IM	*Looking for Pythagoras* R *Kaleidoscopes, Hubcaps, and Mirrors* R
pyramids		*Filling and Wrapping* IM	*Looking for Pythagoras* R
base plans/top, side, and front views	See also *Ruins of Montarek* ©2004 IM	*Filling and Wrapping* R	*Thinking With Mathematical Models* R *Frogs, Fleas, and Painted Cubes* R

Geometry (cont.)			
	Grade 6	**Grade 7**	**Grade 8**
spatial visualization	*Shapes and Designs* I *Covering and Surrounding* I *How Likely Is It?* I See also *Ruins of Montarek* ©2004 IM	*Stretching and Shrinking* R *Filling and Wrapping* R	*Thinking With Mathematical Models* R *Looking for Pythagoras* R *Frogs, Fleas, and Painted Cubes* R *Kaleidoscopes, Hubcaps, and Mirrors* R *The Shapes of Algebra* R
Transformations			
reflections	*Shapes and Designs* I	*Accentuate the Negative* I	*Frogs, Fleas, and Painted Cubes* I *Kaleidoscopes, Hubcaps, and Mirrors* IM *The Shapes of Algebra* R
rotations	*Shapes and Designs* I		*Kaleidoscopes, Hubcaps, and Mirrors* IM
translations		*Stretching and Shrinking* I *Accentuate the Negative* I	*Frogs, Fleas, and Painted Cubes* I *Kaleidoscopes, Hubcaps, and Mirrors* IM *The Shapes of Algebra* R
combinations of transformations		*Stretching and Shrinking* I	*Kaleidoscopes, Hubcaps, and Mirrors* IM
symmetry	*Shapes and Designs* IM		*Frogs, Fleas, and Painted Cubes* R *Kaleidoscopes, Hubcaps, and Mirrors* R *The Shapes of Algebra* R
constructing symmetric figures			*Kaleidoscopes, Hubcaps, and Mirrors* IM *The Shapes of Algebra* R
dilations		*Stretching and Shrinking* IM *Accentuate the Negative* R	*Kaleidoscopes, Hubcaps, and Mirrors* IM *The Shapes of Algebra* R
algebraic rules/properties for		*Stretching and Shrinking* I	*Kaleidoscopes, Hubcaps, and Mirrors* IM
on a coordinate plane	*Shapes and Designs* I	*Stretching and Shrinking* I *Accentuate the Negative* I	*Looking for Pythagoras* I *Kaleidoscopes, Hubcaps, and Mirrors* IM *The Shapes of Algebra* R

Algebra			
	Grade 6	**Grade 7**	**Grade 8**
Patterns Patterns appear in all 24 units.			
numerical	*Prime Time* I *Bits and Pieces I* I *Shapes and Designs* I *Bits and Pieces II* R *Covering and Surrounding* I *Bits and Pieces III* I *Data About Us* I	*Variables and Patterns* IM *Stretching and Shrinking* R *Comparing and Scaling* R *Accentuate the Negative* R *Moving Straight Ahead* R *Filling and Wrapping* R *Data Distributions* R	*Thinking With Mathematical Models* R *Looking for Pythagoras* R *Growing, Growing, Growing* R *Frogs, Fleas, and Painted Cubes* R *Kaleidoscopes, Hubcaps, and Mirrors* R *Say It with Symbols* R *The Shapes of Algebra* R *Samples and Populations* R
geometric	*Covering and Surrounding* IM	*Variables and Patterns* R *Accentuate the Negative* R *Filling and Wrapping* R	*Thinking With Mathematical Models* R *Frogs, Fleas, and Painted Cubes* R *Say It with Symbols* R
rates of change		*Variables and Patterns* I *Comparing and Scaling* I *Accentuate the Negative* I *Moving Straight Ahead* IM *Filling and Wrapping* R	*Thinking With Mathematical Models* R *Growing, Growing, Growing* R *Frogs, Fleas, and Painted Cubes* R *Say It with Symbols* R *The Shapes of Algebra* R
rules	*Prime Time* I *Bits and Pieces I* I *Shapes and Designs* I *Covering and Surrounding* I	*Variables and Patterns* IM *Comparing and Scaling* R *Moving Straight Ahead* R *Filling and Wrapping* R	*Thinking With Mathematical Models* R *Looking for Pythagoras* R *Growing, Growing, Growing* R *Frogs, Fleas, and Painted Cubes* R *Say It with Symbols* R *Samples and Populations* R
analyzing and making predictions from	*Covering and Surrounding* I *Data About Us* I	*Variables and Patterns* IM *Comparing and Scaling* R *Moving Straight Ahead* R *Filling and Wrapping* R *Data Distributions* R	*Thinking With Mathematical Models* R *Growing, Growing, Growing* R *Frogs, Fleas, and Painted Cubes* R *Say It with Symbols* R *Samples and Populations* R

Algebra (cont.)			
	Grade 6	**Grade 7**	**Grade 8**
functions	*Covering and Surrounding* I	*Variables and Patterns* I *Comparing and Scaling* I *Moving Straight Ahead* IM *Filling and Wrapping* R	*Thinking With Mathematical Models* R *Growing, Growing, Growing* R *Frogs, Fleas, and Painted Cubes* R *Say It with Symbols* R *Samples and Populations* R
Variables/Expressions			
dependent, independent		*Variables and Patterns* I *Moving Straight Ahead* IM	*Thinking With Mathematical Models* R
coefficients		*Variables and Patterns* I *Comparing and Scaling* I *Moving Straight Ahead* IM	*Thinking With Mathematical Models* R *Growing, Growing, Growing* R *Frogs, Fleas, and Painted Cubes* R *Say It with Symbols* R *The Shapes of Algebra* R
like, constant, linear terms		*Variables and Patterns* I *Comparing and Scaling* I *Moving Straight Ahead* IM	*Thinking With Mathematical Models* R *Looking for Pythagoras* R *Frogs, Fleas, and Painted Cubes* R *Say It with Symbols* R *The Shapes of Algebra* R
evaluating		*Variables and Patterns* I *Moving Straight Ahead* IM	
equivalent		*Variables and Patterns* I *Moving Straight Ahead* I	*Growing, Growing, Growing* I *Frogs, Fleas, and Painted Cubes* I *Say It with Symbols* IM *The Shapes of Algebra* R
factored form/ expanded form		*Accentuate the Negative* I *Moving Straight Ahead* IM	*Frogs, Fleas, and Painted Cubes* R *Say It with Symbols* R *The Shapes of Algebra* R
Relationships			
continuous/ discrete		*Variables and Patterns* I *Accentuate the Negative* I *Moving Straight Ahead* IM	*Thinking With Mathematical Models* R *Growing, Growing, Growing* R *Frogs, Fleas, and Painted Cubes* R

Algebra (cont.)			
	Grade 6	**Grade 7**	**Grade 8**
linear	*Data About Us* I	*Variables and Patterns* I *Comparing and Scaling* I *Accentuate the Negative* I *Moving Straight Ahead* IM *Filling and Wrapping* R *Data Distributions* R	*Thinking With Mathematical Models* R *Growing, Growing, Growing* R *Frogs, Fleas, and Painted Cubes* R *Say It with Symbols* R *The Shapes of Algebra* R *Samples and Populations* R
nonlinear	*Covering and Surrounding* I *Data About Us* I	*Variables and Patterns* I *Moving Straight Ahead* I *Filling and Wrapping* I *Data Distributions* I	*Thinking With Mathematical Models* IM *Growing, Growing, Growing* R *Frogs, Fleas, and Painted Cubes* R *Say It with Symbols* R *The Shapes of Algebra* R
inverse		*Variables and Patterns* I *Moving Straight Ahead* I	*Thinking With Mathematical Models* IM *Frogs, Fleas, and Painted Cubes* R *Say It with Symbols* R *The Shapes of Algebra* R
exponential growth/ exponential decay			*Growing, Growing, Growing* IM *Frogs, Fleas, and Painted Cubes* R *Say It with Symbols* R *The Shapes of Algebra* R
quadratic	*Covering and Surrounding* I	*Filling and Wrapping* I	*Frogs, Fleas, and Painted Cubes* IM *Say It with Symbols* R *The Shapes of Algebra* R
slope		*Variables and Patterns* I *Moving Straight Ahead* I	*Thinking With Mathematical Models* IM *Looking for Pythagoras* R *Growing, Growing, Growing* R *The Shapes of Algebra* R
slopes of perpendicular lines/parallel lines		*Moving Straight Ahead* IM	*Looking for Pythagoras* R *The Shapes of Algebra* R
Equations, Linear			
tables for		*Variables and Patterns* I *Comparing and Scaling* I *Moving Straight Ahead* IM	*Thinking With Mathematical Models* R *Growing, Growing, Growing* R *Frogs, Fleas, and Painted Cubes* R *Say It with Symbols* R *The Shapes of Algebra* R

Algebra (cont.)			
	Grade 6	**Grade 7**	**Grade 8**
graphs for		*Variables and Patterns* I *Comparing and Scaling* I *Accentuate the Negative* I *Moving Straight Ahead* IM	*Thinking With Mathematical Models* R *Growing, Growing, Growing* R *Frogs, Fleas, and Painted Cubes* R *Say It with Symbols* R *The Shapes of Algebra* R *Samples and Populations* R
fitting to a graph	*Data About Us* I	*Moving Straight Ahead* IM *Data Distributions* R	*Thinking With Mathematical Models* R *Growing, Growing, Growing* R *Frogs, Fleas, and Painted Cubes* R *Say It with Symbols* R *The Shapes of Algebra* R *Samples and Populations* R
Slope-intercept form $y = mx + b$		*Variables and Patterns* I *Moving Straight Ahead* I *Data Distributions* I	*Thinking With Mathematical Models* IM *Growing, Growing, Growing* R *Say It with Symbols* R *The Shapes of Algebra* R *Samples and Populations* R
Standard form $ax + by = c$			*The Shapes of Algebra* IM
writing		*Variables and Patterns* IM *Comparing and Scaling* R *Moving Straight Ahead* R	*Thinking With Mathematical Models* R *Growing, Growing, Growing* R *Frogs, Fleas, and Painted Cubes* R *Say It with Symbols* R *The Shapes of Algebra* R *Samples and Populations* R
solving with tables		*Variables and Patterns* I *Comparing and Scaling* I *Moving Straight Ahead* IM	*Thinking With Mathematical Models* R *Growing, Growing, Growing* R *Frogs, Fleas, and Painted Cubes* R *Say It with Symbols* R *The Shapes of Algebra* R
solving by graphing		*Variables and Patterns* I *Comparing and Scaling* I *Moving Straight Ahead* IM	*Thinking With Mathematical Models* R *Growing, Growing, Growing* R *Frogs, Fleas, and Painted Cubes* R *Say It with Symbols* R *The Shapes of Algebra* R

Algebra (cont.)			
	Grade 6	**Grade 7**	**Grade 8**
solving symbolically	*Bits and Pieces II* I *Bits and Pieces III* I	*Variables and Patterns* I *Accentuate the Negative* I *Moving Straight Ahead* IM	*Thinking With Mathematical Models* R *Growing, Growing, Growing* R *Frogs, Fleas, and Painted Cubes* R *Say It with Symbols* R *The Shapes of Algebra* R
solving with graphing calculator		*Variables and Patterns* I *Moving Straight Ahead* IM	*Thinking With Mathematical Models* R *Growing, Growing, Growing* R *Frogs, Fleas, and Painted Cubes* R *Say It with Symbols* R *The Shapes of Algebra* R
solving systems of		*Variables and Patterns* I *Moving Straight Ahead* I	*Thinking With Mathematical Models* I *Frogs, Fleas, and Painted Cubes* I *Say It with Symbols* I *The Shapes of Algebra* IM
formulate given a problem situation (and vice versa)		*Variables and Patterns* I *Comparing and Scaling* I *Moving Straight Ahead* IM	*Thinking With Mathematical Models* R *Growing, Growing, Growing* R *Frogs, Fleas, and Painted Cubes* R *Say It with Symbols* R *The Shapes of Algebra* R *Samples and Populations* R
Equations, Quadratic			
writing			*Frogs, Fleas, and Painted Cubes* IM *Say It with Symbols* R
graphs for	*Covering and Surrounding* I		*Frogs, Fleas, and Painted Cubes* IM *Say It with Symbols* R *The Shapes of Algebra* R
solving			*Frogs, Fleas, and Painted Cubes* I *Say It with Symbols* IM *The Shapes of Algebra* R
finding roots			*Frogs, Fleas, and Painted Cubes* I *Say It with Symbols* IM *The Shapes of Algebra* R
inequalities			*The Shapes of Algebra* I

Algebra (cont.)			
	Grade 6	**Grade 7**	**Grade 8**
Equations, Nonlinear			
models		*Variables and Patterns* I *Moving Straight Ahead* I	*Thinking With Mathematical Models* IM *Growing, Growing, Growing* R *Frogs, Fleas, and Painted Cubes* R
cubic			*Thinking With Mathematical Models* I *Frogs, Fleas, and Painted Cubes* I *Say It with Symbols* I
exponential			*Thinking With Mathematical Models* I *Growing, Growing, Growing* IM *Say It with Symbols* R *The Shapes of Algebra* R
inverse			*Thinking With Mathematical Models* IM *Frogs, Fleas, and Painted Cubes* R *Say It with Symbols* R *The Shapes of Algebra* R
of circles			*The Shapes of Algebra* IM
Graphing			
explore shapes of graphs	*Covering and Surrounding* I *Data About Us* I	*Variables and Patterns* IM *Comparing and Scaling* R *Moving Straight Ahead* R see also *Data Around Us* ©2004	*Thinking With Mathematical Models* R *Growing, Growing, Growing* R *Frogs, Fleas, and Painted Cubes* R *Say It with Symbols* R *The Shapes of Algebra* R *Samples and Populations* R
ordered pairs	*Data About Us* I	*Variables and Patterns* IM *Stretching and Shrinking* R *Comparing and Scaling* R *Accentuate the Negative* R *Moving Straight Ahead* R	*Thinking With Mathematical Models* R *Looking for Pythagoras* R *Growing, Growing, Growing* R *Kaleidoscopes, Hubcaps, and Mirrors* R *The Shapes of Algebra* R *Samples and Populations* R
polar coordinates	*Shapes and Designs* IM		

Algebra (cont.)			
	Grade 6	**Grade 7**	**Grade 8**

equations		*Variables and Patterns* I
		Comparing and Scaling I
		Moving Straight Ahead IM
		Data Distributions R
			*Thinking With
			  Mathematical Models* R
			*Growing, Growing,
			  Growing* R
			*Frogs, Fleas, and Painted
			  Cubes* R
			Say It with Symbols R
			Samples and Populations R

inequalities		*Variables and Patterns* I *Moving Straight Ahead* I	*Thinking With Mathematical Models* I *Say It with Symbols* I *The Shapes of Algebra* IM
systems of linear inequalities			*The Shapes of Algebra* IM

using a table	*Covering and
	  Surrounding* I
	Data About Us I
		Variables and Patterns IM
		Comparing and Scaling R
		Moving Straight Ahead R
			*Thinking With
			  Mathematical Models* R
			*Growing, Growing,
			  Growing* R
			*Frogs, Fleas, and Painted
			  Cubes* R

with a graphing calculator		*Variables and Patterns* IM
		Moving Straight Ahead R
			*Thinking With
			  Mathematical Models* R
			*Growing, Growing,
			  Growing* R
			*Frogs, Fleas, and Painted
			  Cubes* R
			Say It with Symbols R

slope		*Variables and Patterns* I
		Comparing and Scaling I
		Moving Straight Ahead IM
			*Thinking With
			  Mathematical Models* R
			*Growing, Growing,
			  Growing* R
			Say It with Symbols R
			The Shapes of Algebra R
			Samples and Populations R

x-intercept		*Variables and Patterns* I
		Moving Straight Ahead IM
			*Thinking With
			  Mathematical Models* R
			*Frogs, Fleas, and Painted
			  Cubes* R
			Say It with Symbols R
			The Shapes of Algebra R
			Samples and Populations R

y-intercept		*Variables and Patterns* I
		Moving Straight Ahead IM
			*Thinking With
			  Mathematical Models* R
			*Growing, Growing,
			  Growing* R
			*Frogs, Fleas, and Painted
			  Cubes* R
			Say It with Symbols R
			The Shapes of Algebra R

Algebra (cont.)		
	Grade 6	**Grade 7**	**Grade 8**
maximum and minimum	*Covering and Surrounding* I	*Filling and Wrapping* I	*Frogs, Fleas, and Painted Cubes* IM *Say It with Symbols* R
systems of equations		*Variables and Patterns* IM *Moving Straight Ahead* R	*Thinking With Mathematical Models* R *Frogs, Fleas, and Painted Cubes* R *Say It with Symbols* R *The Shapes of Algebra* R

Problem Solving Skills

Problem Solving Strategies As a problem solving curriculum, every unit helps students develop a variety of strategies for solving problems such as; building models, making lists and tables, drawing diagrams, and solving simpler problems.

	Grade 6	Grade 7	Grade 8
drawing a diagram	*Bits and Pieces I* R *Shapes and Designs* R *Bits and Pieces II* R *Covering and Surrounding* R *Bits and Pieces III* R *How Likely Is It?* R	*Stretching and Shrinking* R *Accentuate the Negative* R *Filling and Wrapping* R *What Do You Expect?* R	*Thinking With Mathematical Models* R *Looking for Pythagoras* R *Frogs, Fleas, and Painted Cubes* R *Kaleidoscopes, Hubcaps, and Mirrors* R *Say It with Symbols* R
looking for a pattern	*Prime Time* R *Bits and Pieces I* R *Shapes and Designs* R *Bits and Pieces II* R *Covering and Surrounding* R *Bits and Pieces III* R *How Likely Is It?* R *Data About Us* R	*Variables and Patterns* R *Stretching and Shrinking* R *Comparing and Scaling* R *Moving Straight Ahead* R *Filling and Wrapping* R *Data Distributions* R	*Thinking With Mathematical Models* R *Growing, Growing, Growing* R *Frogs, Fleas, and Painted Cubes* R *Kaleidoscopes, Hubcaps, and Mirrors* R *Say It with Symbols* R
making a graph	*Covering and Surrounding* R *Data About Us* R	*Variables and Patterns* R *Stretching and Shrinking* R *Comparing and Scaling* R *Moving Straight Ahead* R *Data Distributions* R	*Thinking With Mathematical Models* R *Growing, Growing, Growing* R *Frogs, Fleas, and Painted Cubes* R *Say It with Symbols* R *The Shapes of Algebra* R *Samples and Populations* R
making a table	*Prime Time* R *Shapes and Designs* R *Covering and Surrounding* R *Bits and Pieces III* R *How Likely Is It?* R *Data About Us* R	*Variables and Patterns* R *Comparing and Scaling* R *Moving Straight Ahead* R *Filling and Wrapping* R *What Do You Expect?* R *Data Distributions* R	*Thinking With Mathematical Models* R *Looking for Pythagoras* R *Growing, Growing, Growing* R *Frogs, Fleas, and Painted Cubes* R *Say It with Symbols* R *Samples and Populations* R

	Grade 6	Grade 7	Grade 8
simulating a problem	*Prime Time* IM *Covering and Surrounding* R *How Likely Is It?* R	*Variables and Patterns* R *Moving Straight Ahead* R *Filling and Wrapping* R *What Do You Expect?* R *Data Distributions* R	*Thinking With Mathematical Models* R *Growing, Growing, Growing* R *Samples and Populations* R
try, check, revise	*Prime Time* IM *Bits and Pieces I* R *Shapes and Designs* R *Bits and Pieces II* R *Covering and Surrounding* R *Bits and Pieces III* R *How Likely Is It?* R *Data About Us* R	*Stretching and Shrinking* R *Comparing and Scaling* R *Accentuate the Negative* R *Moving Straight Ahead* R *Filling and Wrapping* R	*Thinking With Mathematical Models* R *Looking for Pythagoras* R *Growing, Growing, Growing* R *Frogs, Fleas, and Painted Cubes* R *Kaleidoscopes, Hubcaps, and Mirrors* R *Say It with Symbols* R *The Shapes of Algebra* R
write an equation	*Shapes and Designs* R *Covering and Surrounding* R	*Variables and Patterns* R *Comparing and Scaling* R *Accentuate the Negative* R *Moving Straight Ahead* R *Filling and Wrapping* R	*Thinking With Mathematical Models* R *Growing, Growing, Growing* R *Frogs, Fleas, and Painted Cubes* R *Say It with Symbols* R *The Shapes of Algebra* R
Reasonableness			
justify answers	*Prime Time* IM *Bits and Pieces I* R *Bits and Pieces II* R *Bits and Pieces III* R *How Likely Is It?* R *Data About Us* R	*Variables and Patterns* R *Stretching and Shrinking* R *Comparing and Scaling* R *Accentuate the Negative* R *Moving Straight Ahead* R *Filling and Wrapping* R *What Do You Expect?* R	*Thinking With Mathematical Models* R *Growing, Growing, Growing* R *Kaleidoscopes, Hubcaps, and Mirrors* R *Say It with Symbols* R *Samples and Populations* R
make and test conjectures	*Prime Time* IM *Bits and Pieces I* R *Shapes and Designs* R *Bits and Pieces II* R *Bits and Pieces III* R *How Likely Is It?* R *Data About Us* R	*Stretching and Shrinking* R *Comparing and Scaling* R *Accentuate the Negative* R *Moving Straight Ahead* R *Filling and Wrapping* R *What Do You Expect?* R *Data Distributions* R	*Thinking With Mathematical Models* R *Looking for Pythagoras* R *Kaleidoscopes, Hubcaps, and Mirrors* R *The Shapes of Algebra* R *Samples and Populations* R
reason from graphs	*Covering and Surrounding* R *Data About Us* R	*Variables and Patterns* R *Stretching and Shrinking* R *Comparing and Scaling* R *Accentuate the Negative* R *Moving Straight Ahead* R *Data Distributions* R	*Thinking With Mathematical Models* R *Growing, Growing, Growing* R *Frogs, Fleas, and Painted Cubes* R *The Shapes of Algebra* R *Samples and Populations* R
validate conclusions using mathematical properties	All units	All units	All units

Communication Student explanations are requested throughout in Problems, in the ACE, and in teacher questioning from the teacher's guides.

Skills in CMP2

Connected Mathematics is committed to the development of mathematical skills—skills that are much more than just quickness with paper-and-pencil algorithms. The overarching goal of CMP discussed on page 2 makes this commitment to skill:

All students should be able to reason and communicate proficiently in mathematics. They should have knowledge of and skill in the use of the vocabulary, forms of representation, materials, tools, techniques, and intellectual methods of the discipline of mathematics, including the ability to define and solve problems with reason, insight, inventiveness, and technical proficiency.

In *Connected Mathematics*, students develop understanding of algorithms and strategies for computing and estimating in a variety of ways. They learn to recognize when an algorithm or strategy applies to a new context and when they can build on the skills and strategies they know in order to develop new strategies. In these processes, students practice skills as an ongoing activity throughout the curriculum.

Students need to know how and when to use paper-and pencil algorithms, mental computation, calculator procedures, and estimation strategies. They need to recognize when an exact answer is required and when an approximate answer is sufficient, and they need a variety of methods for finding an answer. In some situations an approximate answer is sufficient and in these situations a paper-and-pencil algorithm may not be the most efficient (or practical) method. In *Bits and Pieces III* Problem 4.2, Question D(1) students estimate to find a 20% tip for $7.93. It is more efficient for most students to estimate that 10% is about 80 cents so 20% is $1.60 than to multiply 0.20 times 7.93 to obtain $1.57.

Bits and Pieces III • page 53

C. The sales tax in Kadisha's state is 5%. Kadisha says she computes a 15% tip by multiplying the tax shown on her bill by three. For a bill with a tax charge of $0.38, Kadisha's tip is $0.38 × 3 = $1.14.

1. Why does Kadisha's method work?

2. Use a similar method to compute a 20% tip. Explain.

D. When people leave a 15% or 20% tip, they often round up to the nearest multiple of 5 or 10 cents. For example, in Question C, Kadisha might leave a tip of $1.15 rather than $1.14.

1. If Kadisha always rounds up, what is a 20% tip on her bill?

Garden Cafe	
ITEM	AMOUNT
Food	$7.55
5% Tax	.38
TOTAL	$7.93

Students also need to know methods for judging the reasonableness of an answer. For example, to estimate or judge the reasonableness of the answer to the sum $\frac{2}{5}$ and $\frac{1}{3}$, students might argue that $\frac{2}{5}$ is close to but less than $\frac{1}{2}$, and $\frac{1}{3}$ is more than $\frac{1}{4}$ but less than $\frac{1}{2}$. Thus, the answer is more than $\frac{1}{2}$ but less than 1, or about $\frac{3}{4}$.

Skills with the four basic operations on fractions are developed and maintained throughout the curriculum. Students should be able to add two simple fractions quickly by finding a common denominator, but they should also understand why this algorithm works. *Connected Mathematics* helps students build a strong foundation for the development of addition, subtraction, multiplication, and division of fractions. In this phase, the essential building blocks of equivalent fractions, meaning of fractions, models and representation of fractions are developed and used. For example, in *Bits and Pieces I,* students develop an understanding of equivalences. In Problem 2.2 students represent fractions on a number line and use the number line to develop a method of finding equivalent fractions. A portion of this problem is shown on the next page.

Bits and Pieces I • page 22

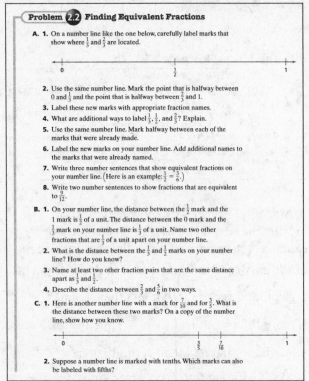

Problem 2.2 Finding Equivalent Fractions

A. 1. On a number line like the one below, carefully label marks that show where $\frac{1}{3}$ and $\frac{2}{3}$ are located.

2. Use the same number line. Mark the point that is halfway between 0 and $\frac{1}{3}$ and the point that is halfway between $\frac{2}{3}$ and 1.

3. Label these new marks with appropriate fraction names.

4. What are additional ways to label $\frac{1}{3}$, $\frac{1}{2}$, and $\frac{2}{3}$? Explain.

5. Use the same number line. Mark halfway between each of the marks that were already made.

6. Label the new marks on your number line. Add additional names to the marks that were already named.

7. Write three number sentences that show equivalent fractions on your number line. (Here is an example: $\frac{1}{2} = \frac{3}{6}$.)

8. Write two number sentences to show fractions that are equivalent to $\frac{9}{12}$.

B. 1. On your number line, the distance between the $\frac{1}{2}$ mark and the 1 mark is $\frac{1}{2}$ of a unit. The distance between the 0 mark and the $\frac{1}{3}$ mark on your number line is $\frac{1}{3}$ of a unit. Name two other fractions that are $\frac{1}{3}$ of a unit apart on your number line.

2. What is the distance between the $\frac{1}{3}$ and $\frac{1}{2}$ marks on your number line? How do you know?

3. Name at least two other fraction pairs that are the same distance apart as $\frac{1}{3}$ and $\frac{1}{2}$.

4. Describe the distance between $\frac{2}{3}$ and $\frac{5}{6}$ in two ways.

C. 1. Here is another number line with a mark for $\frac{7}{10}$ and for $\frac{3}{5}$. What is the distance between these two marks? On a copy of the number line, show how you know.

2. Suppose a number line is marked with tenths. Which marks can also be labeled with fifths?

Students continue to use equivalent fractions to develop understanding of probability, linear functions, and proportional reasoning and to develop algorithms for the operations of fractions.

In *Bits and Pieces II,* students develop and use algorithms to add, subtract, multiply, and divide fractions. After completing this unit, students are given numerous opportunities to use their fraction knowledge and skills in operating with fractions to solve problems in number, geometry, measurement, data analysis probability, and algebra. Below are two examples which illustrate how students continue to use fraction multiplication.

Example 1
Using Fraction Multiplication Skills

In *Bits and Pieces III,* the algorithm of multiplying decimals is connected to multiplying fractions. Here students use their fraction multiplication skills as a strategy to multiply decimals.

Bits and Pieces III • page 22

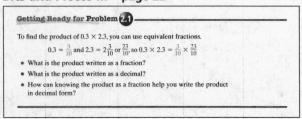

Getting Ready for Problem 2.1

To find the product of 0.3×2.3, you can use equivalent fractions.

$$0.3 = \frac{3}{10} \text{ and } 2.3 = 2\frac{3}{10} \text{ or } \frac{23}{10}, \text{ so } 0.3 \times 2.3 = \frac{3}{10} \times \frac{23}{10}$$

• What is the product written as a fraction?

• What is the product written as a decimal?

• How can knowing the product as a fraction help you write the product in decimal form?

Example 2
Using Fraction Multiplication Skills

Students continue to use their understanding of equivalent fractions to build and consolidate their understanding of new ideas in new contexts. The sequence of the units is carefully chosen with this in mind. For example, in *Stretching and Shrinking,* students use fractional scale factors to find and identify similar figures.

A portion of an Application question and a solution are given below to illustrate continued use of fraction multiplication.

Stretching and Shrinking • page 86

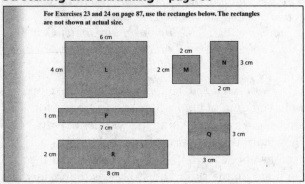

For Exercises 23 and 24 on page 87, use the rectangles below. The rectangles are not shown at actual size.

Stretching and Shrinking • page 87

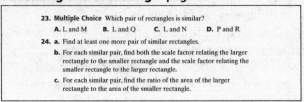

23. Multiple Choice Which pair of rectangles is similar?

A. L and M   **B.** L and Q   **C.** L and N   **D.** P and R

24. a. Find at least one more pair of similar rectangles.

b. For each similar pair, find both the scale factor relating the larger rectangle to the smaller rectangle and the scale factor relating the smaller rectangle to the larger rectangle.

c. For each similar pair, find the ratio of the area of the larger rectangle to the area of the smaller rectangle.

Possible Solution One pair of similar rectangles is Rectangles M and Q. The scale factor from Rectangle Q to Rectangle M is $\frac{2}{3}$. This means that scaling the dimensions of Rectangle Q by $\frac{2}{3}$ results in the dimensions of Rectangle M. Use fraction multiplication to verify that this is the correct scale factor: $3 \text{ cm} \times \frac{2}{3} = 2 \text{ cm}$.

As illustrated with rational numbers above, a similar development is given to integers in *Accentuate the Negative* and irrational numbers in *Looking for Pythagoras.* As students move through the curriculum, they expand their work with the real number system and continue to practice operating with real numbers in a variety of situations.

Proportional reasoning skills are essential to a student's mathematical development. Many problems in K–12 mathematics and beyond call for students to utilize proportional reasoning skills. It is the core idea in being able to write equivalent fractions, in all operations with fractions, in making sense of scales, in similarity, in size transformations, and in solving some linear equations. Students can learn to mimic these skills by learning a new strategy for every skill, but their learning will be much more powerful if they can see an underlying idea and its connections. In the following problem from *Comparing and Scaling,* students are developing proportional reasoning skills. As they solve Problem 2.1, they build on their prior knowledge of fractions and rational numbers.

Comparing and Scaling • page 19

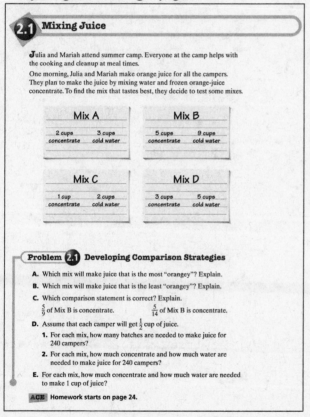

The students of Team 1 used a part-to-whole strategy. They showed that they knew how to find and use percents to make comparisons.

Team 1 Student Work

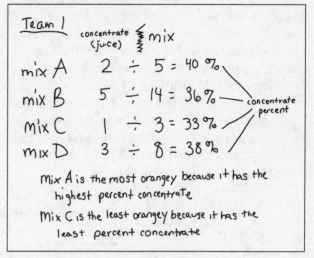

The students on Team 3 used a part-to-part strategy. They gave the ratio in fraction form and then made the numerators the same to make comparisons. They recognized that the smallest denominator shows the mix that is the most "orangey," because it uses the least water per can of concentrate. The work shows that students have flexibility in using fractions, decimals, and percents

Team 3 Student Work

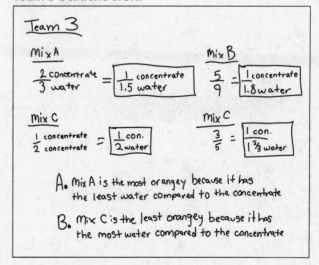

to make their comparisons of ratios.

Knowing when to use a particular operation is also a skill. *Bits and Pieces III* is designed to provide experiences in building algorithms for the four basic operations with decimals, as well as opportunities for students to consider when such operations are useful in solving problems. For example, what features of a problem indicate to the student that division will help solve it? Building this kind of thinking and reasoning supports the development of skill with the algorithms. In Problem 3.1 B. of *Bits and Pieces III,* students need to interpret the problem situation and determine what decimal operation will solve the problem. This skill is practiced as students begin to develop and use algorithms for decimal operations.

Connected Mathematics recognizes that students must have an opportunity to practice skills in a variety of situations throughout the course of their mathematical career. The Connections feature of the ACE Exercises (discussed more on page 43) offers a way for student to continue practicing skills learned in previous units. As a problem-centered curriculum, *Connected Mathematics* provides students the opportunity to use their skills in a wide range of situations that promote higher-order thinking and help students develop problem-solving skills essential to their mathematical future in school and in life. Students explore both problem situations that are purely mathematical and others that are real world. They learn to use what they know to solve contextualized situations and to do computation in "naked" number situations.

Bits and Pieces III • page 37

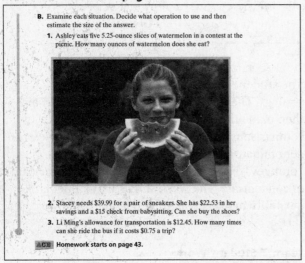

B. Examine each situation. Decide what operation to use and then estimate the size of the answer.

1. Ashley eats five 5.25-ounce slices of watermelon in a contest at the picnic. How many ounces of watermelon does she eat?

2. Stacey needs $39.99 for a pair of sneakers. She has $22.53 in her savings and a $15 check from babysitting. Can she buy the shoes?

3. Li Ming's allowance for transportation is $12.45. How many times can she ride the bus if it costs $0.75 a trip?

ACE Homework starts on page 43.

Algebra in CMP2

Traditionally, an Algebra 1 course focuses on rules or specific strategies for solving standard types of symbolic manipulation problems—usually to simplify or combine expressions or solve equations. For many students, symbolic rules for manipulation are memorized with little attempt to make sense of why they work. They retain the ideas for only a short time. There is little evidence that traditional experiences with algebra help students develop the ability to "read" information from symbolic expression or equations, to write symbolic statements to represent their thinking about relationships in a problem, or to meaningfully manipulate symbolic expressions to solve problems.

In the United States, algebra is generally taught as a stand-alone course rather than as a strand integrated and supported by other strands. This practice is contrary to curriculum practices in most of the rest of the world. Today, there is a growing body of research that leads many United States educators to believe that the development of algebraic ideas can and should take place over a long period of time and well before the first year of high school. Developing algebra across the grades and integrating it with other strands helps students become proficient with algebraic reasoning in a variety of contexts and gives them a sense of the coherence of mathematics.

Developing Algebraic Reasoning in *Connected Mathematics*

The *Connected Mathematics* program aims to expand student views of algebra beyond symbolic manipulation and to offer opportunities for students to apply algebraic reasoning to problems in many different contexts throughout the course of the curriculum. The development of algebra in *Connected Mathematics* is consistent with the recommendations in the NCTM *Principles and Standards for School Mathematics 2000* and most state frameworks.

Algebra in *Connected Mathematics* focuses on the overriding objective of developing students' ability to represent and analyze relationships among quantitative variables. From this perspective, variables are not letters that stand for unknown numbers. Rather they are quantitative attributes of objects, patterns, or situations that change in response to change in other quantities. The most important goals of mathematical analysis in such situations are understanding and predicting patterns of change in variables. The letters, symbolic equations, and inequalities of algebra are tools for representing what we know or what we want to figure out about a relationship between variables. Algebraic procedures for manipulating symbolic expressions into alternative equivalent forms are also means to the goal of insight into relationships between variables. To help students acquire quantitative reasoning skills, we have found that almost all of the important tasks to which algebra is usually applied can develop naturally as aspects of this endeavor. (Fey, Phillips 2005)

There are eight units which focus formally on algebra. Titles and descriptions of the mathematical content for these units are:

Variables and Patterns
Introducing Algebra

Representing and analyzing relationships between variables, including tables, graphs, words, and symbols

Moving Straight Ahead
Linear Relationships

Examining the pattern of change associated with linear relationships; recognizing, representing, and analyzing linear relationships in tables, graphs, words and symbols; solving linear equations; writing equations for linear relationships

Thinking With Mathematical Models
Linear and Inverse Variation

Introducing functions and modeling; finding the equation of a line; representing and analyzing inverse functions

Looking for Pythagoras
The Pythagorean Theorem

Exploring square roots; exploring and using the Pythagorean Theorem, making connections in the coordinate plane among coordinates, slope, and distance

Growing, Growing, Growing
Exponential Relationships

Examining the pattern of change associated with exponential relationships; comparing linear and exponential patterns of growths; recognizing, representing, and analyzing exponential growth and decay in tables, graphs, words and symbols; developing rules of exponents

Frogs, Fleas, and Painted Cubes
Quadratic Relationships

Examining the pattern of change associated with quadratic relationships and comparing these patterns to linear and exponential patterns, recognizing, representing, and analyzing quadratic functions in tables graphs, words, and symbols; determining and predicting important features of the graph of a quadratic functions, such as the maximum/minimum point, line of symmetry, and the x-and y-intercepts; factoring simple quadratic expressions

Say It With Symbols
Making Sense of Symbols

Writing and interpreting equivalent expressions; combining expressions; looking at the pattern of change associated with an expression; solving linear and quadratic equations

Shapes of Algebra
Linear Systems and Inequalities

Exploring coordinate geometry; solving inequalities; solving systems of linear equations and linear inequalities

Early Experiences With Algebraic Reasoning

Even though the first primarily algebra unit occurs at the start of seventh grade, students study relationships among variables in grade 6.

There also are opportunities in 6th and in 7th grade for students to begin to examine and formalize patterns and relationships in words, graphs, tables, and with symbols.

- In *Shapes and Designs* (Grade 6), students explore the relationship between the number of sides of a polygon and the sum of the interior angles of the polygon. They develop a rule for calculating the sum of the interior angle measures of a polygon with N sides.

- In *Covering and Surrounding* (Grade 6), students estimate the area of three different-size pizzas and then relate the area to the price. This problem requires students to consider two relationships: one between the price of a pizza and its area and the other between the area of a pizza and its radius. Students also develop formulas and procedures—stated in words and symbols—for finding areas and perimeters of rectangles, parallelograms, triangles, and circles.

- In *Bits and Pieces I, II* and *III* (Grade 6), students learn, through fact families, that addition and subtraction are inverse operations and that multiplication and division are inverse operations. This is a fundamental idea in equation solving. They use these ideas to find a missing factor or addend in a number sentence.

- In *Data About Us* (Grade 6), students represent and interpret graphs for the relationship between variables, such as the relationship between length of an arm span and height of a person, using words, tables, and graphs.

- In *Accentuate the Negative* (Grade 7), students explore properties of real numbers, including the commutative, distributive, and inverse properties. They use these properties to find a missing addend or factor in a number sentence.

- In *Filling and Wrapping* (Grade 7), students develop formulas and procedures—stated in words and symbols—for finding surface area and volume of rectangular prisms, cylinders, cones, and spheres.

Developing Functions

In a problem-centered curriculum, quantities (variables) and the relationships between variables naturally arise. Representing and reasoning about patterns of change becomes a way to organize and think about algebra. Looking at specific patterns of change and how this change is represented in tables, graphs, and symbols leads to the study of linear, exponential, and quadratic relationships (functions).

Linear Functions

In *Moving Straight Ahead,* students investigate linear relationships. They learn to recognize linear relationships from patterns in verbal, tabular, graphical, or symbolic representations. They also learn to represent linear relationships in a variety of ways and to solve equations and make predictions involving linear equations and functions.

Problem 1.3 illustrates the kinds of questions students are asked when they meet a new type of relationship or function—in this case, a linear relationship. In this problem students are looking at three pledge plans that students suggest for a walkathon.

Whereas many algebra texts choose to focus almost exclusively on linear relationships, in *Connected Mathematics* students build on their knowledge of linear functions to investigate other patterns of change. In particular, students explore inverse variation relationships in *Thinking With Mathematical Models,* exponential relationships in *Growing, Growing, Growing,* and quadratic relationships in *Frogs, Fleas, and Painted Cubes.*

Examples are given below which illustrate the different types of functions students investigate and some of the questions they are asked about these functions. By contrasting linear relationships with exponential and other relationships, students develop deeper understanding of linear relationships.

Inverse Functions

In *Thinking With Mathematical Models,* students are introduced to inverse functions.

Thinking with Mathematical Models • page 32

> **Problem 2.4 Intersecting Linear Models**
>
> **A.** Use the table to find a linear equation relating the probability of rain p to
>
>   **1.** Saturday attendance A_B at Big Fun.
>
>   **2.** Saturday attendance A_G at Get Reel.
>
> **B.** Use your equations from Question A to answer these questions. Show your calculations and explain your reasoning.
>
>   **1.** Suppose there is a 50% probability of rain this Saturday. What is the expected attendance at each attraction?
>
>   **2.** Suppose 400 people visited Big Fun one Saturday. Estimate the probability of rain on that day.
>
>   **3.** What probability of rain would give a predicted Saturday attendance of at least 360 people at Get Reel?
>
>   **4.** Is there a probability of rain for which the predicted attendance is the same at both attractions? Explain.

Exponential Functions

In *Growing, Growing, Growing,* students are given the context of a reward figured by placing coins called rubas on a chessboard in a particular pattern which is exponential. The coins are placed on the chessboard as follows.

Place 1 ruba on the first square of a chessboard, 2 rubas on the second square, 4 on the third square, 8 on the fourth square, and so on, until you have covered all 64 squares. Each square should have twice as many rubas as the previous square.

Moving Straight Ahead • page 9

> - Leanne's sponsors will pay $10 regardless of how far she walks.
> - Gilberto's sponsors will pay $2 per kilometer (km).
> - Alana's sponsors will make a $5 donation plus 50¢ per kilometer.
>
> **Problem 1.3 Using Linear Relationships**
>
> **A. 1.** Make a table for each student's pledge plan, showing the amount of money each of his or her sponsors would owe if he or she walked distances from 0 to 6 kilometers. What are the dependent and independent variables?
>
>   **2.** Graph the three pledge plans on the same coordinate axes. Use a different color for each plan.
>
>   **3.** Write an equation for each pledge plan. Explain what information each number and variable in your equation represents.
>
>   **4. a.** What pattern of change for each pledge plan do you observe in the table?
>
>   **b.** How does this pattern appear in the graph? In the equation?
>
> **B. 1.** Suppose each student walks 8 kilometers in the walkathon. How much does each sponsor owe?
>
>   **2.** Suppose each student receives $10 from a sponsor. How many kilometers does each student walk?
>
>   **3.** On which graph does the point (12, 11) lie? What information does this point represent?
>
>   **4.** In Alana's plan, how is the fixed $5 donation represented in
>
>   **a.** the table?   **b.** the graph?   **c.** the equation?

In this problem students use tables, graphs, and equations to examine exponential relationships and describe the pattern of change for this relationship.

Growing, Growing, Growing • page 7

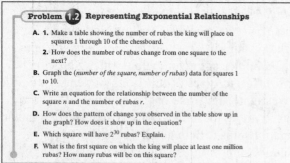

Problem 1.2 Representing Exponential Relationships

A. 1. Make a table showing the number of rubas the king will place on squares 1 through 10 of the chessboard.

   2. How does the number of rubas change from one square to the next?

B. Graph the (*number of the square, number of rubas*) data for squares 1 to 10.

C. Write an equation for the relationship between the number of the square *n* and the number of rubas *r*.

D. How does the pattern of change you observed in the table show up in the graph? How does it show up in the equation?

E. Which square will have 2^{30} rubas? Explain.

F. What is the first square on which the king will place at least one million rubas? How many rubas will be on this square?

Quadratic Functions

In Problem 1.3 from *Frogs, Fleas and Painted Cubes*, students use tables, graphs, and equations to examine quadratic relationships and describe the pattern of change for this relationship.

Frogs, Fleas and Painted Cubes • page 10

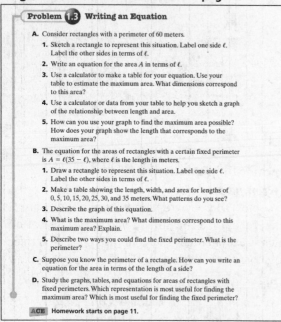

Problem 1.3 Writing an Equation

A. Consider rectangles with a perimeter of 60 meters.

   1. Sketch a rectangle to represent this situation. Label one side ℓ. Label the other sides in terms of ℓ.

   2. Write an equation for the area *A* in terms of ℓ.

   3. Use a calculator to make a table for your equation. Use your table to estimate the maximum area. What dimensions correspond to this area?

   4. Use a calculator or data from your table to help you sketch a graph of the relationship between length and area.

   5. How can you use your graph to find the maximum area possible? How does your graph show the length that corresponds to the maximum area?

B. The equation for the areas of rectangles with a certain fixed perimeter is $A = \ell(35 - \ell)$, where ℓ is the length in meters.

   1. Draw a rectangle to represent this situation. Label one side ℓ. Label the other sides in terms of ℓ.

   2. Make a table showing the length, width, and area for lengths of 0, 5, 10, 15, 20, 25, 30, and 35 meters. What patterns do you see?

   3. Describe the graph of this equation.

   4. What is the maximum area? What dimensions correspond to this maximum area? Explain.

   5. Describe two ways you could find the fixed perimeter. What is the perimeter?

C. Suppose you know the perimeter of a rectangle. How can you write an equation for the area in terms of the length of a side?

D. Study the graphs, tables, and equations for areas of rectangles with fixed perimeters. Which representation is most useful for finding the maximum area? Which is most useful for finding the fixed perimeter?

ACE Homework starts on page 11.

As students explore a new type of relationship, whether it is linear, quadratic, inverse, or exponential, they are asked questions like these:

- *What are the variables? Describe the pattern of change between the two variables.*

- *Describe how the pattern of change can be seen in the table, graph, and equation.*

- *Decide which representation is the most helpful for answering a particular question.* (see Question D in Problem 1.3 in the first column).

- *Describe the relationships between the different representations (table, graph, and equation).*

- *Compare the patterns of change for different relationships. For example, compare the patterns of change for two linear relationships, or for a linear and an exponential relationship.*

Developing Symbolic Reasoning

After students have explored important relationships and their associated patterns of change and ways to represent these relationships, the emphasis shifts to symbolic reasoning.

Equivalent Expressions

Students use the properties of real numbers to look at equivalent expressions and the information each expression represents in a given context and to interpret the underlying patterns that a symbolic statement or equation represents. They examine the graph and table of an expression as well as the context the expression or statement represents. The properties of real numbers are used extensively to write equivalent expressions, combine expressions to form new expressions, predict patterns of change, and to solve equations. *Say It With Symbols* pulls together the symbolic reasoning skills students have developed through a focus on equivalent expressions. It also continues to explore relationships and patterns of change.

Problem 1.1 in *Say It With Symbols* introduces students to equivalent expressions.

Say It With Symbols • page 6

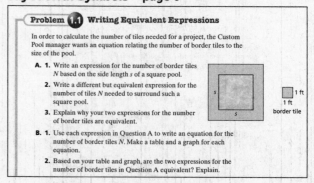

Problem 1.1 Writing Equivalent Expressions

In order to calculate the number of tiles needed for a project, the Custom Pool manager wants an equation relating the number of border tiles to the size of the pool.

A. 1. Write an expression for the number of border tiles *N* based on the side length *s* of a square pool.

   2. Write a different but equivalent expression for the number of tiles *N* needed to surround such a square pool.

   3. Explain why your two expressions for the number of border tiles are equivalent.

B. 1. Use each expression in Question A to write an equation for the number of border tiles *N*. Make a table and a graph for each equation.

   2. Based on your table and graph, are the two expressions for the number of border tiles in Question A equivalent? Explain.

1 ft
1 ft border tile

In Problem 2.1 students revisit Problem 1.3 from *Moving Straight Ahead* (see page 35) to combine expressions. They also use the new expression to find information and to predict the underlying pattern of change associated with the expression.

Say It With Symbols • page 24

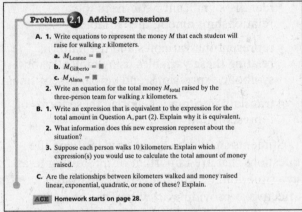

In *Bits and Pieces II* (Grade 6), *Bits and Pieces III* (Grade 6), and *Accentuate the Negative* (Grade 7), students use fact families to find missing addends and factors.

Bits and Pieces II • page 22

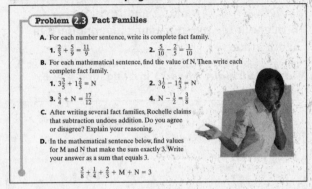

Bits and Pieces III • page 12

C. Find the value of N that makes the mathematical sentence correct. Fact families might help.

1. $63.2 + 21.075 = N$ **2.** $44.32 - 4.02 = N$

3. $N + 2.3 = 6.55$ **4.** $N - 6.88 = 7.21$

Accentuate the Negative • page 30

C. 1. Write a related sentence for each.
  a. $n - {}^{+}5 = {}^{+}35$ **b.** $n - {}^{-}5 = {}^{+}35$ **c.** $n + {}^{+}5 = {}^{+}35$

2. Do your related sentences make it easier to find the value for n? Why or why not?

D. 1. Write a related sentence for each.
  a. ${}^{+}4 + n = {}^{+}43$ **b.** ${}^{-}4 + n = {}^{+}43$ **c.** ${}^{-}4 + n = {}^{-}43$

2. Do your related sentences make it easier to find the value for n? Why or why not?

Bits and Pieces III • page 28

Find the value of N.

17. $3.2 \times N = 0.96$ **18.** $0.7 \times N = 0.042$ **19.** $N \times 3.21 = 9.63$

Solving Equations

Equivalence is an important idea in algebra. A solid understanding of equivalence is necessary for understanding how to solve algebraic equations. Through experiences with different functional relationships, students attach meaning to the symbols. This meaning helps student when they are developing the equation-solving strategies integral to success with algebra.

In CMP, solving linear equation is an algebra idea that is developed across all three grade levels, with increasing abstraction and complexity. In grade six, students write fact families to show the inverse relationships between addition and subtraction and between multiplication and division. The inverse relationships between operations are the fundamental basis for equation solving. Students are exposed early in sixth grade to missing number problems where they use fact families. Below is a description of fact families and a few examples of problems where students use fact families to solve algebraic equations in grades 6 and 7. These experiences precede formal work on equation solving.

In *Variables and Patterns* (Grade 7), students solve linear equations using a variety of methods including graph and tables. As students move through the curriculum, these informal equation-solving experiences prepare them for the formal symbolic methods which are developed in *Moving Straight Ahead* (Grade 7), and revisited throughout the five remaining algebra units in eighth grade.

Moving Straight Ahead • Investigation 4 ACE page 85

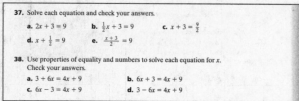

37. Solve each equation and check your answers.

  a. $2x + 3 = 9$ **b.** $\frac{1}{2}x + 3 = 9$ **c.** $x + 3 = \frac{9}{2}$

  d. $x + \frac{1}{2} = 9$ **e.** $\frac{x + 3}{2} = 9$

38. Use properties of equality and numbers to solve each equation for x. Check your answers.

  a. $3 + 6x = 4x + 9$ **b.** $6x + 3 = 4x + 9$

  c. $6x - 3 = 4x + 9$ **d.** $3 - 6x = 4x + 9$

Say It With Symbols (Grade 8), pulls together the symbolic reasoning skills students have developed through a focus on equivalent expressions and on solving linear and quadratic equations.

Say It With Symbols • page 42

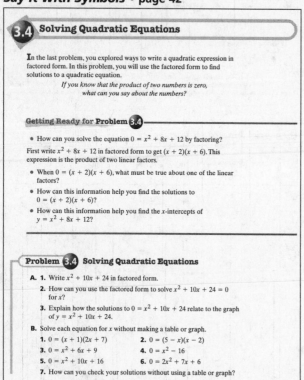

3.4 Solving Quadratic Equations

In the last problem, you explored ways to write a quadratic expression in factored form. In this problem, you will use the factored form to find solutions to a quadratic equation.

> *If you know that the product of two numbers is zero, what can you say about the numbers?*

Getting Ready for Problem 3.4

• How can you solve the equation $0 = x^2 + 8x + 12$ by factoring?

First write $x^2 + 8x + 12$ in factored form to get $(x + 2)(x + 6)$. This expression is the product of two linear factors.

• When $0 = (x + 2)(x + 6)$, what must be true about one of the linear factors?

• How can this information help you find the solutions to $0 = (x + 2)(x + 6)$?

• How can this information help you find the x-intercepts of $y = x^2 + 8x + 12$?

Problem 3.4 Solving Quadratic Equations

A. 1. Write $x^2 + 10x + 24$ in factored form.

  2. How can you use the factored form to solve $x^2 + 10x + 24 = 0$ for x?

  3. Explain how the solutions to $0 = x^2 + 10x + 24$ relate to the graph of $y = x^2 + 10x + 24$.

B. Solve each equation for x without making a table or graph.

  1. $0 = (x + 1)(2x + 7)$ **2.** $0 = (5 - x)(x - 2)$

  3. $0 = x^2 + 6x + 9$ **4.** $0 = x^2 - 16$

  5. $0 = x^2 + 10x + 16$ **6.** $0 = 2x^2 + 7x + 6$

  7. How can you check your solutions without using a table or graph?

Shapes of Algebra (Grade 8), explores solving linear inequalities and systems of linear equations and inequalities.

By the end of Grade 8, students in CMP should be able to analyze situations involving related quantitative variables in the following ways:

• identify variables

• identify significant patterns in the relationships among the variables

• represent the variables and the patterns relating these variables using tables, graphs, symbolic expressions, and verbal descriptions

• translate information among these forms of representation

Students should be adept at identifying the questions that are important or interesting to ask in a situation for which algebraic analysis is effective at providing answers. They should develop the skill and inclination to represent information mathematically, to transform that information using mathematical techniques to solve equations, create and compare graphs and tables of functions, and make judgments about the reasonableness of answers, accuracy, and completeness of the analysis.

Components of CMP2

In addition to 24 student units and accompanying Teacher's Guides, CMP2 includes Additional Practice and Skills Workbooks, Assessment Resources, Teaching Transparencies, Manipulatives Kits, a Special Needs Handbook for Teachers, and a Parent Guide.

The student units, the Additional Practice and Skills Workbooks, and the Assessment Resources are available in Spanish.

Technology components include *ExamView*® CD-ROM (a test generator that includes English and Spanish practice and assessment items), Teacher Express™ CD-ROM (a lesson planning tool with electronic versions of all the print resources), and a Student Activities CD-ROM (interactivities to support conceptual understanding and practice).

In the following pages you will find a detailed discussion of the structure of the student units and the accompanying support found in the Teacher's Guides and other components.

Organization of the Student Units

Connected Mathematics 2 provides eight student units for each grade. One additional unit is offered for each grade from the first edition, ©2004. This allows some flexibility in meeting individual state expectations by allowing the choice of an additional unit when needed. Each unit is organized around an important mathematical idea or cluster of related ideas, such as area and perimeter, operations on fractions, ratio and proportion, linear relationships, or quadratic relationships. The format of the student books promotes student engagement with an exploration of important mathematical concepts and related skills and procedures. Since students develop strategies and conceptual understanding by solving problems and discussing their solutions in class, the books do not contain worked-out examples. Instead the students record their work and explanations as well as their growing understanding of definitions and rules in their notebooks.

The organization and features of each student unit are described below.

Unit Opener

Each unit opens with a set of three focusing questions that reflect the major mathematical goal(s) of the unit. These questions are intended to draw students into the unit, pique their curiosity, and point to the kinds of ideas they will investigate. As the students move through the unit they will encounter these questions either as a problem to explore in class or as homework.

Unit Opener • *Covering and Surrounding*

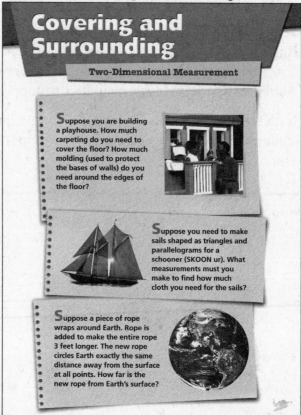

Mathematical Highlights

Next, the unit provides a set of goals, or Mathematical Highlights, that preview the important ideas of the unit. The highlights help students track their progress through the unit and provide parents and guardians with an overview of the mathematical concepts, processes, and ways of thinking developed in the unit.

Mathematical Highlights • *Covering and Surrounding*

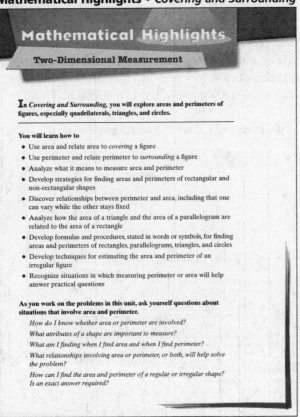

Investigations

The Investigations form the core of a *Connected Mathematics* unit. It is by working through the Investigations that the students develop conceptual understanding, reasoning, and procedural skill. Each Investigation builds toward the mathematical goals. Each unit includes three to five Investigations with the following key elements:

Problem An Investigation includes two to five carefully sequenced Problems. Each Problem is launched by the teacher; then the students explore the Problem individually, in groups, or as a whole class. As students solve the Problems, they uncover important mathematical relationships and develop problem-solving strategies and skills. A summary occurs at the end of each Problem. The teacher pulls the class together and helps students explicitly describe the mathematics of the Problem, ideas, patterns, relationships, and strategies they found and used.

Problem 5.1 • *Covering and Surrounding*

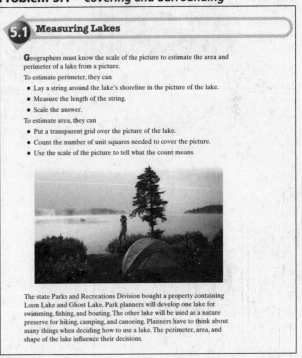

Getting Ready This feature occurs occasionally before a problem. It is intended to be used as part of the launch for the problem. It reviews or introduces the mathematical ideas needed in the problem.

A Getting Ready • *Covering and Surrounding*

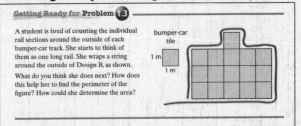

Did You Know? This feature occasionally occurs to present interesting facts related to the context of an investigation.

Did You Know? • *Covering and Surrounding*

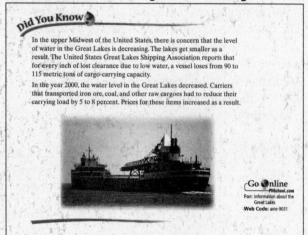

Did You Know

In the upper Midwest of the United States, there is concern that the level of water in the Great Lakes is decreasing. The lakes get smaller as a result. The United States Great Lakes Shipping Association reports that for every inch of lost clearance due to low water, a vessel loses from 90 to 115 metric tons of cargo-carrying capacity.

In the year 2000, the water level in the Great Lakes decreased. Carriers that transported iron ore, coal, and other raw cargoes had to reduce their carrying load by 5 to 8 percent. Prices for these items increased as a result.

Go Online
PHSchool.com
For: Information about the Great Lakes
Web Code: ame-9031

Applications—Connections—Extensions (ACE)

The Problems in each Investigation are followed by a set of exercises meant to be used as homework at the end of each Problem. Students are asked to compare, visualize, model, measure, count, reason, connect, and/or communicate their ideas in writing. To truly own an idea, strategy, or concept, a student must apply it, connect it to what he or she already knows or has experienced, and seek ways to extend or generalize it.

Applications These exercises help students solidify their understanding by providing practice with ideas and strategies that were in the Investigation. Applications contain contexts both similar to and different from those in the Investigation.

Applications • *Covering and Surrounding*

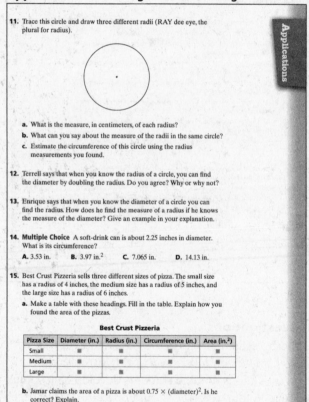

11. Trace this circle and draw three different radii (RAY dee eye, the plural for radius).

   a. What is the measure, in centimeters, of each radius?

   b. What can you say about the measure of the radii in the same circle?

   c. Estimate the circumference of this circle using the radius measurements you found.

12. Terrell says that when you know the radius of a circle, you can find the diameter by doubling the radius. Do you agree? Why or why not?

13. Enrique says that when you know the diameter of a circle you can find the radius. How does he find the measure of a radius if he knows the measure of the diameter? Give an example in your explanation.

14. Multiple Choice A soft-drink can is about 2.25 inches in diameter. What is its circumference?

   A. 3.53 in.   **B.** 3.97 in.^{2} **C.** 7.065 in.   **D.** 14.13 in.

15. Best Crust Pizzeria sells three different sizes of pizza. The small size has a radius of 4 inches, the medium size has a radius of 5 inches, and the large size has a radius of 6 inches.

   a. Make a table with these headings. Fill in the table. Explain how you found the area of the pizzas.

Best Crust Pizzeria

Pizza Size	Diameter (in.)	Radius (in.)	Circumference (in.)	Area (in.^{2})
Small	■	■	■	■
Medium	■	■	■	■
Large	■	■	■	■

   b. Jamar claims the area of a pizza is about $0.75 \times (\text{diameter})^2$. Is he correct? Explain.

Connections A powerful learning strategy is to connect new knowledge to prior learning. The Connections section of the homework provides this opportunity. This section also provides continued review of concepts and skills across the grades. For example, the Connections in *Covering and Surrounding,* a unit on measurement, contain practice with operations on decimals and fractions. Connections can also connect to "real-world problems." Often these are problems that contain original data sets. For example, in *Moving Straight Ahead,* a unit on linear relationships, there are connections to sports records.

Connections • *Covering and Surrounding*

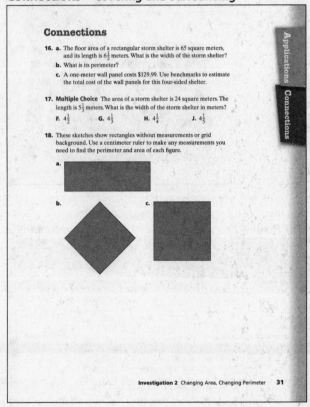

Extensions These exercises may provide a challenge for students to think beyond what is covered in the Problems in class, provide an interesting excursion "side ways" that looks at related mathematical ideas, foreshadow mathematics in future units or pursue an interesting application.

Extensions • *Covering and Surrounding*

Mathematical Reflections

At the end of each Investigation, students are asked to reflect on what they have learned. A set of questions helps students organize their thoughts and summarize important concepts and strategies. After thinking about the questions and sketching their own ideas, students discuss the questions with their teacher and their classmates and then write a summary of their findings.

Mathematical Reflections • *Covering and Surrounding*

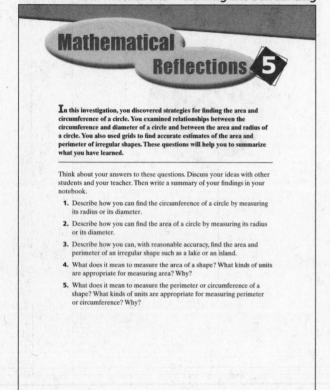

Mathematical Reflections 5

In this investigation, you discovered strategies for finding the area and circumference of a circle. You examined relationships between the circumference and diameter of a circle and between the area and radius of a circle. You also used grids to find accurate estimates of the area and perimeter of irregular shapes. These questions will help you to summarize what you have learned.

Think about your answers to these questions. Discuss your ideas with other students and your teacher. Then write a summary of your findings in your notebook.

1. Describe how you can find the circumference of a circle by measuring its radius or its diameter.

2. Describe how you can find the area of a circle by measuring its radius or its diameter.

3. Describe how you can, with reasonable accuracy, find the area and perimeter of an irregular shape such as a lake or an island.

4. What does it mean to measure the area of a shape? What kinds of units are appropriate for measuring area? Why?

5. What does it mean to measure the perimeter or circumference of a shape? What kinds of units are appropriate for measuring perimeter or circumference? Why?

Unit Project

At least four units at each grade level include projects. Projects are typically introduced at the beginning of a unit and formally assigned at the end. A list of projects is given on page 53. Projects are open-ended tasks that provide opportunities for students to engage in independent work and to demonstrate their broad understanding of the mathematics of the unit.

Unit Project • *Covering and Surrounding*

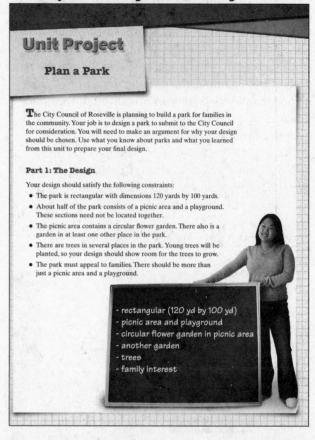

Unit Project

Plan a Park

The City Council of Roseville is planning to build a park for families in the community. Your job is to design a park to submit to the City Council for consideration. You will need to make an argument for why your design should be chosen. Use what you know about parks and what you learned from this unit to prepare your final design.

Part 1: The Design

Your design should satisfy the following constraints:

- The park is rectangular with dimensions 120 yards by 100 yards.
- About half of the park consists of a picnic area and a playground. These sections need not be located together.
- The picnic area contains a circular flower garden. There also is a garden in at least one other place in the park.
- There are trees in several places in the park. Young trees will be planted, so your design should show room for the trees to grow.
- The park must appeal to families. There should be more than just a picnic area and a playground.

- rectangular (120 yd by 100 yd)
- picnic area and playground
- circular flower garden in picnic area
- another garden
- trees
- family interest

Unit Project (continued) • *Covering and Surrounding*

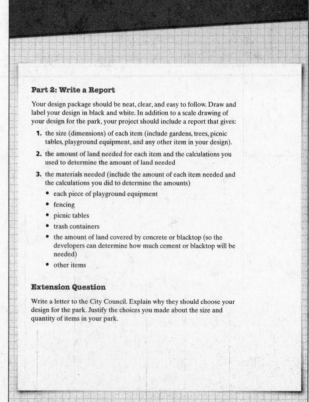

Part 2: Write a Report

Your design package should be neat, clear, and easy to follow. Draw and label your design in black and white. In addition to a scale drawing of your design for the park, your project should include a report that gives:

1. the size (dimensions) of each item (include gardens, trees, picnic tables, playground equipment, and any other item in your design).

2. the amount of land needed for each item and the calculations you used to determine the amount of land needed

3. the materials needed (include the amount of each item needed and the calculations you did to determine the amounts)
   - each piece of playground equipment
   - fencing
   - picnic tables
   - trash containers
   - the amount of land covered by concrete or blacktop (so the developers can determine how much cement or blacktop will be needed)
   - other items

Extension Question

Write a letter to the City Council. Explain why they should choose your design for the park. Justify the choices you made about the size and quantity of items in your park.

Looking Back and Looking Ahead

This feature provides a review of the "big" ideas and connections in the unit. It includes problems that allow students to demonstrate their understanding, explain their reasoning, summarizing and connecting what they have learned within and across units.

Looking Back and Looking Ahead
Covering and Surrounding

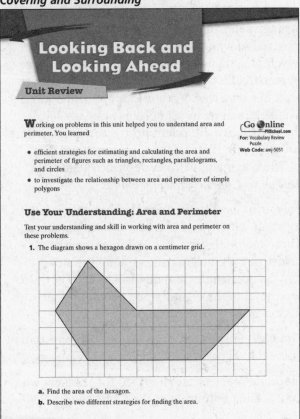

Looking Back and Looking Ahead *(continued)*
Covering and Surrounding

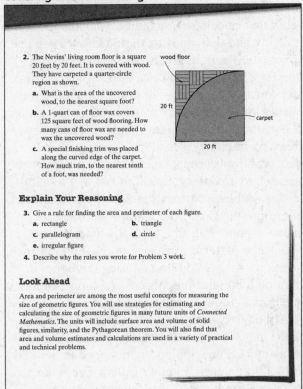

Glossary

Although students are encouraged to develop their own definitions and examples for key terms, a glossary in English and Spanish is provided at the back of each student book. Glossaries can serve as a guide for the student, the teacher, and parents as students develop understanding of key ideas and strategies.

Glossary • *Covering and Surrounding*

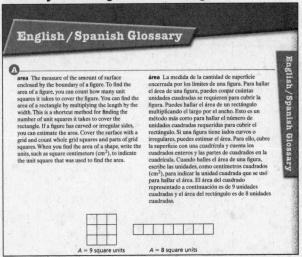

Technology for Students

Connected Mathematics was developed with the belief that calculators should be available to students, and that students should know *when* and *how* to use them. In grade 6, students need standard, four-function calculators. Students use four-function calculators to simplify complicated calculations and explore patterns in computations.

For some units in grades 7 and 8, students need access to graphing calculators with table and statistical-display capabilities. Graphing calculators are used to investigate functions and as a tool for solving problems. Students use graphing calculators to explore the shape and features of graphs of linear, exponential, and quadratic functions as well as the patterns of change in the tables of such functions. And in addition to using symbolic solution methods, students use graphing-calculator tables and graphs to solve equations.

Although computers are not required for any of the investigations, applets are provided for many units. Some applets are designed to be used during the Launch, Explore, Summarize sequence and some can be used at various stages of the instruction, including additional practice with the ideas in the unit. The applets are provided on the Student Activities CD-ROM.

Manipulatives

In *Connected Mathematics*, manipulatives are used only when they can help students develop understanding of mathematical ideas. For example, in *Filling and Wrapping,* students find all the different rectangular arrangements possible for a given number of cubes. They find the surface area of each arrangement by creating a net (covering) for the arrangement that exactly fits, with no overlap or underlap. They then identify the arrangements that require the least and the most material to wrap. This activity sets the stage for developing the ideas of surface area and volume of rectangular prisms. Most of the manipulatives used in *Connected Mathematics* are commonly available, and many schools may already have them. Included are rulers, protractors, angle rulers, cubes, square tiles, counters, spinners, and dice.

The two manipulatives described below are unique to *Connected Mathematics.*

Polystrips are plastic strips that can be pieced together with brass fasteners to form polygons. These manipulatives are used in grade 6 to investigate the relationship among the side lengths of triangles and quadrilaterals. They also are useful in the eighth grade geometry unit, *Kaleidoscopes, Hubcaps, and Mirrors.*

The CMP Shapes Set® is a set of polygons used in grade 6 to explore sides, angles, and tilings.

Blackline masters are provided for teachers who do not have Polystrips or the CMP Shapes Set.

A list of materials for each unit is found in the Unit Introduction of each Teacher's Guide.

In *Connected Mathematics*, teachers are an integral part of the learning process. From the beginning, the authors have viewed *Connected Mathematics* as a curriculum for both students and teachers. *Connected Mathematics* provides teachers with ways to think about and enact problem-centered teaching that address the following aspects of instruction.

The CMP Instructional Model

Problem-centered teaching opens the mathematics classroom to exploring, conjecturing, reasoning, and communicating. The *Connected Mathematics* teacher materials are organized around an instructional model that supports this kind of teaching. This model is very different from the "transmission" model in which teachers tell students facts and demonstrate procedures and then students memorize the facts and practice the procedures. The CMP model looks at instruction in three phases: launching, exploring, and summarizing. The following text describes the three instructional phases and provides the general kinds of questions that are asked. Specific notes and questions for each problem are provided in the Teacher's Guides.

Launch 1.1

In the first phase, the teacher launches the problem with the whole class. This involves helping students understand the problem setting, the mathematical context, and the challenge. The following questions can help the teacher prepare for the launch:

- *What are students expected to do?*

- *What do the students need to know to understand the context of the story and the challenge of the problem?*

- *What difficulties can I foresee for students?*

- *How can I keep from giving away too much of the problem solution?*

The launch phase is also the time when the teacher introduces new ideas, clarifies definitions, reviews old concepts, and connects the problem to past experiences of the students. It is critical that, while giving students a clear picture of what is expected, the teacher leaves the potential of the task intact. He or she must be careful to not tell too much and consequently lower the challenge of the task to something routine, or to cut off the rich array of strategies that may evolve from a more open launch of the problem.

Explore 1.1

The nature of the problem suggests whether students work individually, in pairs, in small groups, or occasionally as a whole class to solve the problem during the explore phase. The Teacher's Guide suggests an appropriate grouping. As students work, they gather data, share ideas, look for patterns, make conjectures, and develop problem-solving strategies.

It is inevitable that students will exhibit variation in their progress. The teacher's role during this phase is to move about the classroom, observing individual performance and encouraging on-task behavior. The teacher helps students persevere in their work by asking appropriate questions and providing confirmation and redirection where needed. For students who are interested in and capable of deeper investigation, the teacher may provide extra questions related to the problem. These questions are called Going Further and are provided in the explore discussion in the Teacher's Guide. Suggestions for helping students who may be struggling are also provided in the Teacher's Guide. The explore part of the instruction is an appropriate place to attend to *differentiated learning*.

The following questions can help the teacher prepare for the explore phase:

- *How will I organize the students to explore this problem? (Individuals? Pairs? Groups? Whole class?)*

- *What materials will students need?*

- *How should students record and report their work?*

- *What different strategies can I anticipate they might use?*

- *What questions can I ask to encourage student conversation, thinking, and learning?*

- *What questions can I ask to focus their thinking if they become frustrated or off-task?*

- *What questions can I ask to challenge students if the initial question is "answered"?*

As the teacher moves about the classroom during the explore, she or he should attend to the following questions:

- *What difficulties are students having?*

- *How can I help without giving away the solution?*

- *What strategies are students using? Are they correct?*

- *How will I use these strategies during the summary?*

Summarize 1.1

It is during the summary that the teacher guides the students to reach the mathematical goals of the problem and to connect their new understanding to prior mathematical goals and problems in the unit. The summarize phase of instruction begins when most students have gathered sufficient data or made sufficient progress toward solving the problem. In this phase, students present and discuss their solutions as well as the strategies they used to approach the problem, organize the data, and find the solution. During the discussion, the teacher helps students enhance their conceptual understanding of the mathematics in the problem and guides them in refining their strategies into efficient, effective, generalizable problem-solving techniques or algorithms.

Although the summary discussion is led by the teacher, students play a significant role. Ideally, they should pose conjectures, question each other, offer alternatives, provide reasons, refine their strategies and conjectures, and make connections. As a result of the discussion, students should become more skillful at using the ideas and techniques that come out of the experience with the problem.

If it is appropriate, the summary can end by posing a problem or two that checks students' understanding of the mathematical goal(s) that have been developed at this point in time. Check

For Understanding questions occur occasionally in the summary in the Teacher's Guide. These questions help the teacher to assess the degree to which students are developing their mathematical knowledge. The following questions can help the teacher prepare for the summary:

- *How can I help the students make sense of and appreciate the variety of methods that may be used?*

- *How can I orchestrate the discussion so that students summarize their thinking about the problem?*

- *What questions can guide the discussion?*

- *What concepts or strategies need to be emphasized?*

- *What ideas do not need closure at this time?*

- *What definitions or strategies do we need to generalize?*

- *What connections and extensions can be made?*

- *What new questions might arise and how do I handle them?*

- *What can I do to follow up, practice, or apply the ideas after the summary?*

Organization of the Teacher's Guide

The extensive field-testing of *Connected Mathematics* has helped produce teacher materials that are rich with field teachers' successful strategies, classroom dialogues and questions, and examples of student solutions and reasoning (see page 31). The Teacher's Guide for each unit contains a discussion of the mathematics underlying the Investigations, mathematical and problem-solving goals for each Investigation, connections to other units, in-depth teaching notes, and an extensive assessment package.

The teacher materials are designed as a resource to facilitate teaching *Connected Mathematics*. The features and organization of the Teacher's Guide are described on the next page.

Unit Introduction

Teachers can use the material in the Unit Introduction to prepare for teaching the unit. The following features are included in this section:

Unit Introduction
- **Goals of the Unit**
- **Developing Students' Mathematical Habits**

The Mathematics in the Unit
- **Overview**
- **Summary of the Investigations**
- **Mathematics Background** A detailed description designed to assist teachers in understanding the content

Content Connections to Other Units
A chart highlighting how the big ideas of the unit connect to ideas from previous and future units

Planning for the Unit
- **Pacing Suggestions and Materials**
- **Vocabulary**

Program Resources
- **Components**
- **Technology**

Assessment Summary (see page 54)
- **Ongoing Informal Assessment**
- **Formal Assessment**
- **Correlations to Standardized Tests**

Launching the Unit
- **Using the Unit Opener**
- **Using the Mathematical Highlights**
- **Introducing the Unit Project**

Teaching Notes

Detailed teaching notes are included for each Investigation. These include the following:

Mathematical Goals for the Investigation

For each problem:

- **Specific Mathematical and Problem-Solving Goals**

- **Detailed Teaching Notes** Includes problem-by-problem discussions with examples of the instructional role of the teacher during the three phases of problem instruction, as well as samples of student responses to questions.

- **Going Further** The explore sections include occasional "Going Further" questions for students who finish early or need another challenge.

- **Check for Understanding** The summary section, when appropriate, may end with questions for the teacher to use to check students' understanding.

Lesson At a Glance This is a two-sided one-page lesson guide for each problem. (A blank At a Glance template is included in each Teacher's Guide to facilitate a teacher's personalization of the lesson plan.) At a Glance contains:

- The mathematical goal for the Problem
- Materials needed for the Problem
- Definitions that need to be addressed
- Key questions for the Launch, Explore, and Summarize phases of the instruction
- Answers to the Problem
- Homework assignment guide

At a Glance • *Shapes and Designs*

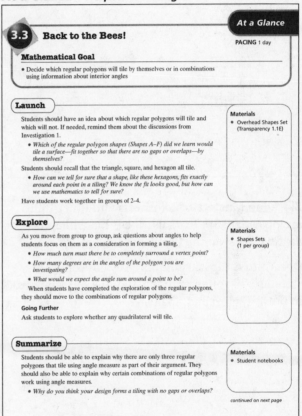

Summarize *continued*

There are eight combinations of regular polygons that will tile so that each vertex has exactly the same pattern of polygons. (note the numbers in parentheses refer to the polygon by side number):

2 octagons and 1 square (8-8-4)
1 square, 1 hexagon, and 1 dodecagon (4-6-12)
4 triangles and 1 hexagon (3-3-3-3-6)
3 triangles and 2 squares (4-3-4-3-3)
1 triangle, 2 squares, and 1 hexagon (4-3-4-6)
1 triangle and 2 dodecagons (3-12-12)
3 triangles and 2 squares (4-3-3-3-4)
2 triangles and 2 hexagons (3-6-3-6)

   Note there are two arrangements with triangles and squares, but depending on the arrangement they produce different patterns.

ACE Assignment Guide for Problem 3.3

Differentiated Instruction
Solutions for All Learners

Core 11, 12

Other *Connections* 18, 19; *Extensions* 25; unassigned choices from previous problems

Adapted For suggestions about adapting ACE exercises, see the CMP *Special Needs Handbook*.

Answers to Problem 3.3

A. 1.

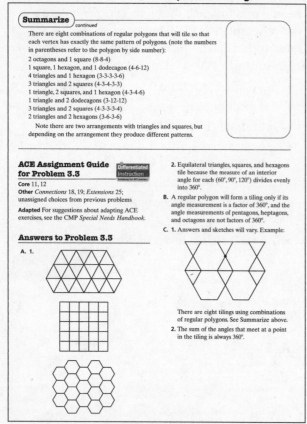

2. Equilateral triangles, squares, and hexagons tile because the measure of an interior angle for each (60°, 90°, 120°) divides evenly into 360°.

B. A regular polygon will form a tiling only if its angle measurement is a factor of 360°, and the angle measurements of pentagons, heptagons, and octagons are not factors of 360°.

C. 1. Answers and sketches will vary. Example:

There are eight tilings using combinations of regular polygons. See Summarize above.

2. The sum of the angles that meet at a point in the tiling is always 360°.

Blackline Masters of Labsheets and other things are provided. Students use these blackline masters as they work on the problem sets.

Descriptive Glossary/Index Key concepts are summarized, often with illustrations or examples, in both English and Spanish.

Support Materials for Teachers

In addition to the Teacher's Guide for each unit, there are several resources that are designed to assist teachers. They are:

Teaching Transparencies support problems from the student books. All the Getting Ready features are available on transparencies.

Parent materials for *Connected Mathematics* include a parent letter for each unit with the goals of the unit and examples of worked problems, as well as a website for parents to help with homework for each unit.

Special Needs Handbook for Teachers includes suggestions for adapting instruction, examples of modified problems and ACE exercises from the student books, and assessment items for each unit.

Assessment Resources include blackline masters for Partner Quizzes, Check-Ups, Unit Tests, multiple- choice items, Question Bank, Notebook Check and Self-Assessment for each grade level. They are also available in Spanish and on a CD-ROM.

Additional Practice and Skills Workbook for each grade level provides practice exercises for each investigation as well as additional skills practice to reinforce student learning.

Technology A Student Activities CD-ROM provides activities to enhance and support classroom learning in the Problems/Investigations of the Student books.

Teacher Express™ CD-ROM includes lesson planning software, the Teacher's Guide pages, and all the teaching resources.

Exam View® Test Generator CD-ROM includes all the items from the Assessment Resources and the Additional Practice and Skills Workbook in both English and Spanish. Items can be edited electronically and saved. Many items are dynamic, and can be used to create multiple versions of practice sheets.

Assessment

Assessment Dimensions

Assessment in *Connected Mathematics* is an extension of the learning process, as well as an opportunity to check what students can do. For this reason, the assessment is multidimensional, giving students many ways to demonstrate how they are making sense of the mathematics.

The *Curriculum and Evaluation Standards for School Mathematics* (NCTM, 1989), the *Assessment Standards for School Mathematics* (NCTM, 1995), and the *Principles and Standards for School Mathematics* (NCTM 2000) provide guidelines that describe mathematics education in schools, not only in terms of mathematical objectives, but in terms of the methods of instruction, the processes used by students in learning and doing mathematics, and the students' disposition towards mathematics. Assessment in *Connected Mathematics* is designed to collect data concerning these three dimensions of student learning:

Content knowledge

Assessing content knowledge involves determining what students know and what they are able to do.

Mathematical disposition

A student's mathematical disposition is healthy when he or she responds well to mathematical challenges and sees himself or herself as a learner and inventor of mathematics. Disposition also includes confidence, expectations, and metacognition (reflecting on and monitoring one's own learning).

Work habits

A student's work habits are good when he or she is willing to persevere, contribute to group tasks, and follow tasks to completion. These valuable skills are used in nearly every career. To assess work habits, it is important to ask questions, such as *"Are the students able to organize and summarize their work?"* and *"Are the students progressing in becoming independent learners?"*

The NCTM *Principles and Standards 2000* reinforces the CMP philosophy on assessment. Its Assessment Principle states:

Assessment should support the learning of important mathematics and furnish useful information to both teachers and students.

Assessment Tools

Connected Mathematics provides a variety of tools for student assessment. These assessments fall into three broad categories:

Checkpoints

Some of the assessment tools—such as ACE assignments, notebooks, Mathematical Reflections, and the Unit Review—give teachers and students an opportunity to check student understanding at key points in the unit. Checkpoints help students solidify their understanding, determine the areas that need further attention, and help teachers make decisions about whether students are ready to move on. The "Check for Understanding" feature of some summaries gives students and teachers an additional checkpoint on students progress.

Surveys of Knowledge

Check-ups, quizzes, unit tests, and projects provide teachers with a broad view of student knowledge both during a unit and at the end of a unit.

Observations

The curriculum provides teachers with numerous opportunities to assess student understanding by observing students during group work and class discussions. This form of assessment is important, since some students are better able to show understanding in verbal situations than in formal, written assignments. Teachers may also receive feedback from parents—who may comment on their child's enthusiasm or involvement with a particular problem—and from students who may observe that another student's method is more efficient or useful, or who may offer an important observation, conjecture or extension. More information about each assessment tool is given below.

Checkpoints

ACE By assigning ACE exercises as homework, teachers can assess each student's developing knowledge of concepts and skills.

Notebooks and Notebook Checklist Many teachers require their students to keep organized notebooks, which include homework, notes from class, vocabulary, and assessments. Each unit includes a checklist to help students organize their notebooks before they turn them in for teacher feedback. Teachers can also assess student understanding during their study of the unit by examining their work or summaries for particular problems.

Mathematical Reflections A set of summarizing questions, called Mathematical Reflections, occurs at the end of each investigation. These questions can help teachers assess students' developing conceptual knowledge and skills in the investigation. (See page 70.)

Looking Back and Looking Ahead This Unit Review feature includes two to four problems that ask students to explain their reasoning. Collectively, the pieces have students summarize and connect what they have learned within and across units. This component can be used as a review, helping students to stand back and look at the "big" ideas and connections in the unit. (See page 71.)

Surveys of Knowledge

Check-ups Check-ups are short, individual assessment instruments. Check-up questions tend to be less complex and more skill-oriented than questions on quizzes and unit tests. These questions provide insight into student understanding of the baseline mathematical concepts and skills of the unit. Student responses to Check-ups can help teachers plan further instruction for the unit.

Partner Quizzes Each unit has at least one partner quiz. Quiz questions are richer and more challenging than checkup questions. Many quiz questions are extensions of ideas students explored in class. These questions provide insight into how students apply the ideas from the unit to new situations. The quizzes were created with the following assumptions:

- Students work in pairs.

- Students are permitted to use their notebooks and any other appropriate materials, such as calculators.

- Pairs have an opportunity to submit a draft of the quiz for teacher input. They may then revise their work and turn in the finished product for assessment.

Unit Tests Each unit includes a test that is intended to be an individual assessment. The test informs teachers about a student's ability to apply, refine, modify, and possibly extend the mathematical knowledge and skills acquired in the unit. Some of the questions draw on ideas from the entire unit, while others are smaller, focusing on a particular idea or concept. Some of the questions are skill oriented, while others require students to demonstrate problem-solving abilities and more in-depth knowledge of the unit concepts. Teachers can use holistic scoring techniques and rubrics that take into account the many dimensions addressed by the test.

Self-Assessment After every unit, students complete a self-assessment, summarizing the mathematics they learned in the unit and the ideas with which they are still struggling. The self-assessment also asks students to provide examples of what they did in class to add to the learning of the mathematics. The goal of this activity is to have students reflect on their learning. For many students, self-assessment is a new experience, and they may struggle with this at first. However, by receiving feedback from teachers and using other students' work as models, students can learn to reflect on their own progress in making sense of mathematics.

Project At least four units in each grade include projects that can be used to replace or supplement the unit test. Projects give teachers an opportunity to assign tasks that are more product/performance-based than those on traditional tests. Project tasks are typically open-ended and allow students to engage in independent work and to demonstrate broad understanding of ideas in the unit. Through students' work on the projects, teachers can gather information about their disposition toward mathematics. Project guidelines, student examples, and scoring rubrics appear in the Assessment Resources section for the unit. The table on the next page gives locations and descriptions of projects by grade level.

Question Bank A bank of questions is provided for each unit. Teachers may use these questions as homework problems, as class investigation problems, or as replacements for quiz and check-up questions. Some of these questions give students an additional opportunity to work on problems similar to those in the unit, while others extend the ideas of the unit.

Unit Projects by Grade

Grade 6	Grade 7	Grade 8
Prime Time **PROJECT: My Special Number** Students choose a "special number" and use all they have learned in the unit to describe mathematical properties and real-world applications or occurrences of their numbers. **Shapes and Designs** **PROJECT: What I Know About Shapes and Designs** Students create representations of what they have learned about various polygons, the relationships of their sides and angles, and where these shapes can be found in their world. **Covering and Surrounding** **PROJECT: Plan a Park** Students create scale drawings for a park that meet given constraints and submit a written proposal highlighting the features of their parks. **Bits and Pieces III** **PROJECT: Ordering From a Catalog** Students select items from a catalog and fill out an order form, calculating shipping, tax and discounts. **Data About Us** **PROJECT: Is Anyone Typical?** Students apply what they have learned in the unit to gather, organize, analyze, interpret, and display information about the "typical" middle school student.	**Stretching and Shrinking** **PROJECT: Shrinking or Enlarging Pictures** Students shrink or enlarge a drawing or photograph by hand. They then analyze the relationships among the lengths, areas, and angle measurements of the original and those of the new drawing. **PROJECT: All-Similar Shapes** Students analyze a variety of shapes to determine which shapes are always mathematically similar to other shapes of the same kind. **Comparing and Scaling** **PROJECT: Paper Pool** Students look at several simplified pool tables to determine the number of hits a ball will make before it goes into a pocket and the pocket in which it lands. They use their results to make predictions for other tables. **Filling and Wrapping** **PROJECT: Package Design Contest** Students design packages for table-tennis balls, calculate the costs of their packages, and justify the designs of their packages. **What Do You Expect?** **PROJECT: The Carnival Game** Students design carnival games and analyze the probabilities of winning and the expected values. They then write a report explaining why their games should be included in the school carnival. **Accentuate the Negative** **PROJECT: Dealing Down** Students apply what they have learned to a game. They then write a report explaining their strategies and their use of mathematics. **Moving Straight Ahead** **PROJECT: Conducting an Experiment** Students collect data about dripping water or rebounding balls and make predictions based on their data.	**Growing, Growing, Growing** **PROJECT: Half-Life** Students use cubes to simulate the radioactive decay of a substance and estimate its half-life. They then create a new situation involving radioactive decay and design and carry out their own simulation. **Kaleidoscopes, Hubcaps and Mirrors** **PROJECT: Making Tessellations** Students analyze the symmetries of various tessellations and create their own tessellations. **PROJECT: Making a Wreath and a Pinwheel** Students make an origami wreath and transform it into a pinwheel. They investigate and describe the symmetries of their creation at various stages. **Say It With Symbols** **PROJECT: Finding the Surface Area of Red Stacks** Students find the volume and surface area of stacks and rods. They look for patterns and then apply what they have learned about writing algebraic expressions to describe patterns that they observe and verify the equivalence of those expressions. **Samples and Populations** **PROJECT: Estimating a Deer Population** Students simulate a capture-recapture method for estimating deer populations, conduct some research, and write a report.

Observations

Group Work Many problems provide the opportunity to observe students as they "do mathematics," applying their knowledge, exhibiting their mathematical disposition, and displaying their work habits as they contribute to group tasks.

Class Discussions The summary portion of each problem and the Mathematical Reflections at the end of each Investigation provide ongoing opportunities to assess students' understanding through class discussions.

Students and Parents Through Self Assessments, Partner Quizzes, group work, and class discussions, students have the opportunity to observe and assess their own content knowledge, mathematical disposition, and work habits. Parents may also observe their child's progress, disposition, and work habits and share them with the teacher.

Summary of Assessment Dimensions and Tools

Finally, this chart summarizes the assessment tools in *Connected Mathematics* and the dimensions addressed by each assessment item.

Assessment Tool	Assessment Dimension		
	Content Knowledge	**Mathematical Disposition**	**Work Habits**
Checkpoints			
ACE	✔	✔	✔
Notebooks	✔	✔	✔
Mathematical Reflections	✔	✔	✔
Looking Back and Looking Ahead	✔	✔	✔
Surveys of Knowledge			
Check-ups	✔		
Partner Quizzes	✔	✔	✔
Unit Tests	✔		
Self-Assessment	✔	✔	✔
Project	✔	✔	✔
Question Bank	✔		
Observations			
Group Work	✔	✔	✔
Class Discussions	✔	✔	✔
Students and Parents	✔	✔	✔

Implementing CMP2

Because a problem-centered curriculum (see page 6 this document) may be quite different from that experienced by teachers, administrators, and parents/guardians in the community, a shift to such a curriculum is likely to generate excitement as well as some discomfort and uncertainty.

Some concerns are shared by all members of the community. For example, in the early stages of the adoption process, members of the community will want to know what data already exists that describes the effectiveness of *Connected Mathematics*. As the implementation proceeds, members of the community have an interest in the results of a well-planned, ongoing evaluation of student learning in their school district. Some issues are of greater concern to administrators and teachers than to parents/guardians. For example, administrators will need to plan for multi-faceted professional development to support teachers through different stages of the curriculum, from novice first-year implementers to confident, successful teachers of CMP. Teacher concerns include the need for ongoing support, not just in the initial implementation stage, but also in the development of a thriving culture of professionals working together to make decisions about improving the teaching and learning of mathematics in the building.

Parent/guardian concerns are likely to focus on two issues: how to help their students be successful in a curriculum that looks unfamiliar to them, and how CMP students will make the transition to the expectations of high school mathematics classes. Below are some suggestions for informing, engaging, and preparing all members of the community as they tackle the work necessary—from early evidence gathering and planning to well-supported, successful implementation of CMP.

Curriculum by itself is not enough, but a good curriculum in the hands of a good teacher, with support of the administration, the local community, and long-term professional development, can provide the kinds of mathematical experiences that support higher levels of mathematical performance for all students.

Initial Stages

Connected Mathematics is standards based and problem centered. Adopting and implementing a standards-based mathematics curriculum can be a major step for school districts.

To replace a curriculum often described as "a mile wide and an inch deep," standards-based mathematics curricula focus attention on a core agenda of important and broadly useful mathematical ideas. To replace instruction that asks students to watch passively and imitate teacher demonstrations of routine computational techniques, these curricula engage students in challenging mathematical investigations that help them construct solid understanding of key ideas and confident ability to solve tough mathematical problems. (James Fey, *Montgomery Gazette,* Montgomery County, September 10, 1999)

Standards-based curricula such as CMP are organized differently than traditional mathematics textbooks. Parents and teachers are accustomed to textbooks that have examples followed by pages of skill exercises. Many teachers are accustomed to instruction characterized by working a few examples for the whole class, then assigning a set of practice problems to be done independently by the students. Although most teachers supplement this pattern by occasionally having students solve non-routine problems, such activity is not at the core of their curriculum or central to their teaching.

Not only do the standards-based textbooks look different but they also ask teachers, students, and parents to play different roles. In the traditional curriculum teachers actively demonstrate solutions, students somewhat passively observe, parents and guardians support and supervise practice, and the textbook provides examples. In CMP classrooms, students actively investigate problems and develop solutions, and teachers question, challenge, and orchestrate explicit summaries of the mathematics being learned. Parents and guardians will benefit from information about the rationale for the organization and sequencing of the problems, the role of ACE questions and Looking Back/Looking Ahead activity in each unit, and the way that student notebooks are designed to capture a student's evolving knowledge of a topic. Standards-based curricula like CMP look different and make different demands on all members of the community.

Connected Mathematics teaches mathematics through a sequence of connected problems in an inquiry-based classroom. This a major shift away from a focus on developing skills and procedures to a focus on mathematics as a set of relationships between a specialized symbolic language, concepts, facts, ways of thinking, and procedures. School districts can make this shift and smooth the implementation of CMP by following guidelines for orchestrating the process. Bay et al. (1999) list ten important factors related to successful selection and implementation of standards-based mathematics curricula. These include: administrative support; opportunities to study and pilot the curricula; time for daily planning and interaction with colleagues; knowledge of appropriate assessment techniques and tools; ongoing communication with parents; and articulation with colleagues at the elementary and secondary level.

Before adopting *Connected Mathematics,* school personnel should take time to:

Gather Evidence

- Seek reviews of research that might answer the question, *"Why do we want to change? What more do we want for our students that the current texts do not provide?"*

- Seek reviews of research that might guide evaluation of textbooks, rather than rely solely on the data provided by the publisher. *"What are we seeking in a new text, and how can we find helpful and reliable information?"*

- Know how middle school students in your district are performing on state or local assessments. Ask teachers to provide input into where they see strengths and/or weaknesses in the current curriculum materials. Involve a parent group in reviewing the evidence and establishing goals. *"Are there particular areas of strength or weakness?"*

- Seek, or request from the publisher, data describing the effectiveness of CMP or any other curricula under consideration. *"Was the curriculum used in a district like ours?"*

- Create an evaluation plan for measuring student achievement. Plan to collect baseline data the year before implementation. *"What is our goal for student achievement? What realistically can we expect? How will we evaluate student's achievement over the long run?"*

- Seek information about the preparation and confidence level of teachers in the district. *"What support is there for teachers either in the textbook itself or from other sources?"*

Garner Administrative and Community Support

- Superintendents, principals, and other administrators as well as school boards and parents must have access to clear information about the CMP materials. The administration and staff need a well-developed strategy for providing the mechanisms through which such information is made available to the school board and to parents and kept updated.

- Familiarize principals and other administrators with CMP. They should know the rationale for the change in curricular emphasis and how CMP will better meet the needs of students.

- Work with parents to gain support. Some districts have found that a parent/community advisory group is helpful. Involving parents during the conceptualization of the implementation can avoid misunderstandings later.

- Work with teachers to gain support. Request and respect input from all teachers.

Address Important Issues and Questions

- *How does CMP "fit" with district and state frameworks?* Correlate curriculum goals with local/state requirements and assessment instruments.

- *How does CMP handle basic skills?* The answer to this question, as well as the evidence of the impact of the curriculum on students' basic skills, is readily available. The results consistently show that CMP

students do as well as, or better than, non-CMP students on tests of basic skills. And CMP students outperform non-CMP students on tests of problem solving ability, conceptual understanding, and proportional reasoning. (See www.math.msu.edu/CMP: Research and Reports.)

- *Will CMP be used in all grades (6–8), with all levels of students? Will students with learning difficulties or reading difficulties find it too difficult?* (See pages 87–99.)

- *If algebra is offered as a separate course in middle school, will CMP be used in this course? If so, how does CMP support the development of algebra concepts and skills?* (See www.msu.edu/CMP: Curriculum.) Experiences of other schools that are successfully using CMP in 6–8, including for an 8th grade algebra class, can be a powerful resource. (See www.math.msu.edu/CMP: Research and Reports: State and District Data.)

- *How will students make the transition from CMP to high school? Who should be involved in making a transition plan?*

- *Are students coming out of our K–5 ready for CMP? Should we involve elementary teachers in making a transition plan from upper elementary to CMP?*

Enable Teacher Buy-In

The size, composition of staff, and past experiences of the school district and staff will determine how the following actions are handled.

- Consider piloting units before adopting the entire curriculum (if feasible).

- Develop an implementation plan. *Will all students (and teachers) begin using the materials at the same time? Will they be phased in over the course of two to three years?*

- Establish plans for long-term professional development that coincides with the implementation schedule (more on this in the next section).

- Designate teacher or building leaders responsible for scheduling/planning professional development.

Districts need to take early action on the preceding items. The best professional development plans have gone astray because schools did not take the time to share with the key players in their districts the rationale for a new curriculum focus and to develop a wide base of support. If a district committee, representing all the key players, has collected evidence about CMP as suggested above, then any questions from parents or teachers can be honestly and rationally answered. If the adoption process has been transparent, then the community will have had an opportunity to ask questions and seek reassurance.

The Principal's Role

The successful principal of a school has many roles to play as he/she interacts with all members of the school's community. Broadly speaking, with district level administrators the interaction is about the business of managing a school, with teachers the interaction is about the teaching and learning of a curriculum, and with parents the interaction is about the success of individual children. When CMP is adopted, the principal who takes the time to become knowledgeable about the curriculum will be better able to support teachers and answer parent questions. Becoming knowledgeable is the first step.

Becoming Knowledgeable About the Curriculum

The District Textbook Committee In the initial stages of selection and adoption, the district committee will have sought out evidence of reasons for adopting CMP, of current achievement levels of students, of the success of CMP in other districts, and of the preparation of teachers to implement CMP. The district committee will also have sought answers to questions about how students with disabilities or gifted and talented students succeed in CMP, about the place of Algebra in CMP, and about the issues to be considered in helping students make successful transitions from elementary school to middle school, and from middle school to high school. This evidence and current thinking about these issues should be shared with principals so that they feel confident that a thoughtful decision has been made, and so that they can relate achievement goals and teacher preparation to their own buildings. The building principal needs to be knowledgeable so that he/she can speak confidently and supportively about the curriculum and related issues to teachers and to parents.

Since CMP is standards based and problem centered, the principal will need to find time to understand what these two terms mean (see pages 3, 6–7, 27–28 of this document), and how this kind of curriculum looks in a classroom when it is being successfully implemented. In this role the principal is acting like the principal teacher in the building, asking questions such as, *"What research backs this kind of approach? What does this kind of curriculum mean for student groupings? What role does the teacher have? What help will the teacher need in organizing this kind of classroom? What can I do to help with classroom issues?"* If the principal is knowledgeable about the curriculum and teacher needs, then more teachers are apt to "buy-in" to the curriculum.

After becoming knowledgeable about the curriculum, the principal will also have to consider his/her role in professional development activities. There is only so much a principal can do to learn about a curriculum by reading about it. The principal who actively participates in professional development will be much more knowledgeable, and will be perceived as much more supportive by teachers.

Being Supportive of Teachers

When teachers attend professional development activities to help themselves successfully implement CMP, they learn first hand about the mathematics in the units, about the connections among units, and about how problems are sequenced to develop mathematical ideas. They also learn about pedagogical aspects of the curriculum: why the curriculum is organized the way it is, what the teacher role is in the launch phase of a lesson, in the student exploration of a problem, and in the crucial summary phase. The principal who is present at professional development activities with teachers is likely to be attending less to the actual mathematics under study than to the perceived needs of teachers. Just as teachers learn to ask questions about what their students have learned and how they can be more supportive of student learning, so the principal can ask, *"Do some of my building's teachers seem to need more help with the mathematics than others? How can I get them this help? Who seems fearful or resistant? Why is that? What can I do to increase the confidence of the teachers in my building that they can implement CMP? Do they need more information? More encouragement?"*

As the building leader, the principal is the point person when questions come from district administrators and from parents/guardians. And as such the principal can be an advocate for teachers. When professional support for teachers needs district approval, the principal can make a case for what is needed; or when concerned parents/guardians have questions about a teacher's unfamiliar classroom practices, the principal can knowledgeably reassure the parent and support the teacher.

It is important to be supportive of teachers in the evaluation process. When both teachers and principals understand the goals of CMP and how these goals are achieved, then the process of evaluating teachers has integrity and validity that would be lacking if the principal had one picture in mind and the teacher had another. Evaluation based on mutually valued goals and practices fosters professionalism. The opportunity for a principal to observe and evaluate how CMP is being enacted in a particular classroom, can be an opportunity to reinforce the common goals and aspirations that the building personnel share.

Communicating with Parents/Guardians

The building principal knows better than any other district administrator what his part of the district looks like, which parents he/she can expect to be involved in building activities, and which he/she can expect to have questions or concerns. The district can make general plans and suggestions to involve parents/ guardians, but the principal is uniquely placed to know best which plans are good fits for his/her school. From the list of suggestions below, or from others, each principal must make a wise selection so that parents and guardians feel included, and can be more supportive of their students' success in learning mathematics.

Involving Parents/Guardians

Some parents and guardians may have been involved in the initial stages described above. But most will only become aware that a new curriculum has been adopted after the fact. They may have questions about why CMP was adopted, why it looks different from traditional textbooks, and what evidence there is of student success. As mentioned above, the unfamiliarity of the problem-centered approach may be an obstacle that parents need help in overcoming. These are questions that a district committee that has done its work well in the initial stages can answer, or can arrange to have answered in a variety of ways.

Conscientious parents have always been concerned about their children's middle school education. Their concerns usually have two distinct foci:

- *What is my role in helping my child be successful now?*
- *How well does this class prepare my child for high school mathematics and for post-secondary education?*

Keeping Parents and Guardians Informed

Parents/guardians need to understand the goals of the program. Administrators and teachers can help them do this by keeping them informed, early and often, about both long-term and unit goals. They should know that the primary goal of CMP is to have students make sense of mathematical concepts, become proficient with basic skills, and communicate their reasoning and understanding clearly. The concepts and topics that students study should be familiar to parents/guardians, but the problem-centered textbooks may not make the particular topic or skill as explicit as the associated student work and reflections will. Parents and guardians need advice and help in making good use of their students' classwork as a resource.

The emphasis in reasoning and communication may be less familiar. Curriculum leaders and teachers can help parent/guardians understand why reasoning and communication are valued and that the program provides many opportunities to demonstrate students' progress in these areas. There are many specific ways that a district can gain the support of parents and guardians, and keep them informed:

Form a Community Advisory Group The group should be composed of knowledgeable and strong advocates for the program. The committee should consist of parents and guardians, teachers, university people (if there is a university in the area), business people (particularly those who appreciate the need for critical thinking) and administrators. This group will play a crucial role in the early stages of implementation, and less of a role as the success of CMP speaks for itself.

Present Information to the Community As implementation matures, a district might create a pamphlet for parents and guardians, including the results of district evaluation studies showing how well CMP students did on state tests.

Conduct Parent Workshops These can be helpful at the beginning of the school year, and at different stages of the implementation during the year. Topics to be discussed might include: overarching goals, evidence of effectiveness of CMP, specific mathematical information, the instructional model, mathematical expectations for students by the end of the year and the end of the program, the use of calculators, and transition to high school. An effective strategy for conducting these workshops is to engage parents/guardians in a problem from one of the student units, so they can experience first hand how understanding and skill are developed in CMP. These workshops might be tailored to fit specific concerns such as use of calculators and other technology, and how this affects learning or the particular mathematical goals of a unit that is about to start.

Send an Introductory Letter An introductory letter complements the Parent Workshops outlined above. A sample letter is included in the *Parent Guide for CMP2*.

Send a Parent/Guardian Letter As students begin a new unit, the teacher can send a letter to parents/guardians stating the goals of the unit and suggesting questions that parents/ guardians can ask their children. The *Parent Guide for CMP2* contains a sample parent/guardian letter for each unit.

Send Home Parent/Guardian Handbooks A district can create and send home handbooks addressing the mathematics in units and suggesting ways that parents/guardians can help their children.

Send Home Newsletters A newsletter is an excellent way to highlight the mathematics students are studying. A newsletter might include student work, stories about student insights, summaries of rich class discussions, or other evidence of achievement. If your district already has a community newsletter, then it may be possible to include news from the mathematics classroom in the newsletter.

Inform Parents/Guardians of Resources CMP provides a parent Web site offering both background information and specific mathematical help to parents seeking to assist their students with homework. See www.math.msu.edu/CMP/parents and PHSchool.com.

Tutoring Labs Conduct a tutoring lab after school to reassure parents that additional help is available to students for homework. In one CMP district, a mathematics lab is held two days a week after school. Students sign up with their mathematics teacher to attend, and must bring with them work to do, such as homework, redoing a past assignment, organizing their notebooks, working on vocabulary lists or projects, or studying for a test or quiz. Copies of student units and Teacher's Guides and other materials and tools typically found in the classroom are available in the lab.

Teachers' Guides Make a copy of the Teacher's Guides, with answers removed, available in the school library for checking out.

Parent and Guardian Role: A Supportive Parent CMP Web site

Parents/guardians are an invaluable resource to the district if their knowledge, good intentions, and caring can be channeled to be compatible with the problem-centered approach of CMP.

"The first teachers are the parents, both by example and conversation."

–Lamar Alexander.

In helping children learn, a parent/guardian's first goal should be to assist children in figuring out as much as they can for themselves. They can help by asking questions that guide, without telling what to do. Good questions and good listening will help children make sense of mathematics, build self-confidence, and encourage mathematical thinking and communication. A good question opens up a problem and supports different ways of thinking about it. A list of such questions is available at the CMP Parent Web site (www.math.msu.edu/CMP/parents), along with background information about the curriculum. In addition to general information and advice, the Web site also offers specific mathematical information. A vocabulary list, with examples to illuminate meaning and use of new vocabulary, and examples of solutions of homework exercises are just two of the aids that parents/guardians will find at this site. This site can help parents/guardians to have meaningful mathematical conversations with their children.

Parents/guardians are some of the knowledgeable experts in their child's universe. Their expertise may be in the mathematical ideas, or in the learning process itself. They can help with homework by learning how to scaffold a problem for a child, without taking away all the gains to be made from the student's individual struggle.

Selecting and Implementing Connected Mathematics Units in Grades 6, 7, and 8

The units in Connected Mathematics were identified, developed, and carefully sequenced to help students build deep understanding and skill with important mathematical ideas. Once a unit has been taught, then the understandings and procedural skills developed in the unit are used in succeeding units to build unerstandings of new concepts and skills. Therefore the order in which the units are listed for each grade is the recommended order for teaching the units. (See page 15 for the units in the recommended teaching order.)

Two typical implementation plans are:

- A three-year plan–one grade level at a time, and

- All three grades in the first year.

If the school chooses to implement all three grades in the first year, it is important for teachers at each grade level to know what mathematics is taught the previous year and the succeeding year. Most of the material that is taught in 6th grade occurs in most 6th grade textbooks. However, if something is taught in CMP that was not taught the previous year in your school, then the 7th grade teachers may need to add an extra lesson or two to cover this topic. The same procedures should be done by 6th and 8th grade teachers. After the first year, there should be very little, if any, adjustments needed to the curriculum that is prescribed for each grade.

How many units a school teaches per grade level is difficult to predict. Length of class periods, number of days spent on instruction, district obectives, and the background of incoming 6th grade students are just some of the variables. Class periods vary from 40 to 90 minutes across the country. The difference of ten minutes can mean as much as one extra unit being taught.

Transition to High School

Planning for the transition to high school should be part of any successful implementation plan. As soon as the district has made the decision to adopt CMP in middle school, teachers and administrators at the high school level must take time to get to know the CMP curriculum and what students can be expected to do, long before CMP students start arriving in 9th grade. Likewise, parents and guardians of middle school students, especially those going into 8th grade, should be included in the information loop about this transition.

Presently a trend throughout the country is to make the study of algebra a goal for all eighth grade students. If successful, these students may go on to take calculus, or other advanced mathematics classes, in their senior year of high school. Certainly, it is a worthy goal for all students to become more proficient in algebra and to include more algebra in the curriculum prior to high school. Indeed, the Connected Mathematics Project was funded by the National Science Foundation and designed by its authors with this as one of its goals.

One strategy, tried by some schools, is to move the traditional Algebra 1 course to 8th grade. However, experience has shown that many eighth grade students fail a traditional Algebra 1 course, and must repeat it in high school. A more promising strategy, recommended by the NCTM *Principles and Standards 2000,* is the development of algebraic ideas over a longer period of time, well before the first year of high school, to better prepare students to deal with abstraction and symbols. This philosophy is consistent with the way that algebra is taught in other countries. The NCTM *Principles and Standards* guided the development of the algebra strand in the Connected Mathematics Project.

Algebra Goals in CM

Algebra is developed in all three grades of *Connected Mathematics.* By the end of Grade 8, CMP students have studied an impressive array of algebraic ideas and skills. Most students should be able to meet the following goals.

Patterns of Change—Functions

- Identify and use variables to describe relationships between quantitative variables in order to solve problems or make decisions.

- Recognize and distinguish among patterns of change associated with linear, inverse, exponential, and quadratic functions.

Representation

- Construct tables, graphs, symbolic expressions, and verbal descriptions and use them to describe and predict patterns of change in variables.

- Move easily among tables, graphs, symbolic expressions, and verbal descriptions.

- Describe the advantages and disadvantages of each representation and use these descriptions to make choices when solving problems.

- Use linear and inverse equations and inequalities as mathematical models of situations involving variables.

Symbolic Reasoning

- Connect equations to problem situations.

- Connect solving equations in one variable to finding specific values of functions.

- Solve linear equations and inequalities and simple quadratic equations using symbolic methods.

- Find equivalent forms of many kinds of equations, including factoring simple quadratic equations.

- Use the distributive and commutative properties to write equivalent expressions and equations.

- Solve systems of linear equations.

High School Math Courses for CMP Students

If the high school offers a standards-based mathematics curriculum, then the approach will be compatible with CMP. High school and middle school teachers need to communicate with each other about what CMP students can do coming out of Grade 8 in order to make sure that there is no unintended duplication or unexpected gap. It may well be the case that students who have been successful in CMP in 8th grade can skip the first year of the high school program. Obviously this decision can only be made based on knowledge of both programs, and the best guides are the teachers involved.

If the high school in the district is still offering a traditional Algebra 1, Geometry, Algebra 2 sequence, then, based on what courses are available at 9th grade, and on how successful a particular student has been in 8th grade CMP, there are several options for the district to consider. Two options are outlined below. In neither of these options is it necessary for a student who has been successful in the algebra units in CMP to spend a valuable year of high school in a traditional Algebra 1 class.

Students who have been successful in the CMP algebra units will have met and mastered many of the ideas and skills that are part of a traditional Algebra 1. But, they also will have done very much more than this in their study of algebra in CMP. Their experience will have been a coherent functions approach to important mathematical relationships, especially linear, exponential, inverse proportion, and quadratic,—including solving linear, exponential, and quadratic equations, and inverse and direct proportions. Therefore, CMP algebra units are an excellent preparation for a traditional functions-based approach in Algebra 2. Because of this extensive and thorough study of algebraic ideas in CMP, many students entering a high school with a traditional curriculum in place may successfully proceed to Algebra 2.

If, on examining what is expected of students coming out of 8th grade CMP, teachers in a high school offering the traditional curriculum see skills which they believe are integral to Algebra 1 and which CMP students have not met, then they may create a short "patch" which can be added to the 8th grade CMP units. However, Algebra 2 textbooks typically include a lot of review of Algebra 1, and, therefore, would review and supplement what students know from CMP.

In summary, many students who complete all 8 algebra units of CMP2 and meet other district criteria may successfully proceed to a traditional Geometry and/or Algebra 2 course. Whatever options are offered to students entering 9th grade after a successful CMP experience in 8th grade, they should be based on teacher input, knowledge of the CMP curriculum and the high school curriculum, data about student achievement—particularly on algebraic topics—and input from all the professionals involved.

Professional Development

Successful Long-Term Professional Development

Experience and research suggest that effective professional development models have some common characteristics. Effective, professional development

- Begins prior to curriculum implementation and continues through several years of implementation.

- Is centered on the particular curriculum that will be/has been adopted, in this case, CMP.

- Develops teachers' knowledge of mathematics and pedagogy.

- Models and reflects good mathematical pedagogy.

- Addresses teacher concerns about change.

- Involves teachers in reflecting and planning for improvement.

- Creates strong leadership.

- Includes a plan for training new teachers as they join the district.

- Reflects strong support from administration and parents.

- Establishes an expectation among teachers of working together to learn from and with each other during and after the formal professional development has ceased.

Change in itself can be problematic and the changes for some teachers associated with using any standards-based curricula are significant. The Concerns-Based Adoption Model (CBAM) (Hall & Hord, 1987, Hord, et al. 1987, Loucks-Horsley, 1989, Friel and Gann, 1993) offers help in addressing these issues. Teachers may need help moving through levels of concern, from non-awareness to ownership of new ideas, from a focus on themselves and their own needs to a focus on their students' learning needs. The stages of concern can be described as

- Self-concerns—*What is this new change and how will it affect me?*

- Task-oriented concerns—*How do I implement this change? What do I need to do to make this change happen with my students?*

- Impact-oriented concerns—*How are my students learning? Are they learning more and are they learning better? How do I work with others who are also implementing these new ideas?*

Progressing through these stages of concern while one is implementing CMP takes time—two to three years is a good target.

The change process is ongoing with different needs surfacing during the period of professional development and implementation. Early in the professional development component, time is needed to address teachers' concerns about implementing CMP. In the beginning these concerns may tend to focus on management, grading issues, special needs students, tracking, skills, transitions to high school, etc. While these issues are important and should be addressed, they can divert attention from content and instruction. These concerns can be addressed gradually during the first phase of professional development. Let teachers have time to get their concerns on the table early in the process and be assured that these concerns will be addressed. Many of the concerns become less urgent as the teachers engage in studying the mathematics and sharing their knowledge with colleagues. These experiences help teachers integrate previous teaching practice with new expectations.

Good professional development to support a standards-based curricula like CMP weaves mathematics, pedagogy, and assessment together. To make significant changes, professional development must address teachers' stages of concerns and concurrently provide opportunities for growth. Growth should focus on

- Developing a deeper understanding and broader view of mathematics (mathematical knowledge).

- Strengthening teachers' pedagogical knowledge (teaching & learning).

- Exploring assessment aligned with inquiry-based instructional strategies (assessment).

Professional development must be based on sound criteria and principles that have evolved from research and been verified in experience. The research discussed above as well as other research described by Loucks-Horsley et. al (1996), the extensive experiences of the CMP authors and staff, and the *Professional Standards for Teaching Mathematics* (NCTM 1991) serve as important references for our professional development design. Examples of professional development plans are available on the CMP Web site. See www.math,msu.edu/CMP: Professional Development.

Three components—content, teaching and learning, and assessment—are core areas of the professional development model and each comes to the foreground at critical times during the professional development. Below is a rationale for the components that need to be included, and an order of inclusion that has been successful.

Mathematical Knowledge

An effective professional development model associated with preparing for and implementing CMP begins with an emphasis on mathematical content, with supporting pedagogy being modeled by the professional development leader. Teachers need to be comfortable with the mathematics embedded in the problems in order to begin to examine how the materials can be taught to reach their full potential.

Teachers benefit from examining the complete picture of how mathematical ideas build on previous ideas and how those ideas in turn provide the foundation for the mathematics in later units and in subsequent grades. Even teachers who have taught mathematics for some time will find that ideas that they have accepted without questioning are presented in a new light, one that illuminates both meaning and connections to other mathematics and to other uses of the mathematics. There is value in trying to see mathematical ideas as they are first encountered by a student, rather than reproducing what has been stored in memory. Asking, *"How do I know this? Why does it make sense?"* are not questions that teachers typically take the time to ask about familiar mathematics, yet they are at the core of understanding how students learn new material.

Good instructional decisions and practice rely on deep understanding of the mathematics that is embedded in the problems. We suggest that developing the mathematics of the units in early professional development be given primary focus, with any pedagogical discussions focusing only on how to help students learn the mathematics. Discussions of management and assessment are more effective if they occur toward the end of the early professional development. First developing mathematical and pedagogical content knowledge keeps the professional development from becoming mired in discussions of issues that as yet have no real basis for a substantive conversation.

Teaching and Learning

Having developed a better understanding of the mathematics within CMP, the focus of professional development can shift teaching and learning to the foreground. Teachers need to experience inquiry-based pedagogy in their professional development so that it will serve as a model for their own teaching. They also need to be involved in sufficient conversations about teaching problem-centered materials to feel comfortable during implementation.

More in-depth work on instruction after teachers have experience in teaching units is needed and is very effective in improving teacher practice. The idea that teachers should be encouraged to reflect upon, revise, and refine their initial understandings of the mathematics in a unit, and of ways to teach, after practical experience parallels the learning process that is expected of students. It is worth noting that when the focus shifts to pedagogy, teachers continue to develop their own understanding of the mathematics through conversations that analyze student work and assess student understanding.

While the teacher and student books serve an important role in helping the teacher implement the curriculum within their classroom, teachers also need time away from their classroom to talk with peers and to fully investigate the potential of the curriculum.

Assessment

Once teachers have begun using inquiry-based instruction in CMP, it becomes clear that traditional forms of assessment that focus only on skills may be insufficient to gauge the depth and breadth of student learning. CMP offers a variety of forms of assessment to support teachers, including embedded assessment, which may be unfamiliar to teachers.

Orchestrating different types of assessment requires new skills for teachers and should be included in the professional development program. Figuring out how to assess and how to grade assessments is a concern of teachers that tends to arise as implementation progresses. Therefore the time for assessment to be an emphasis in professional development is after teachers have experienced some of the curriculum. Equally important is the influence of assessment as evidence to promote teacher reflection and decision making. For example, with support and experience, teachers begin to see assessment as data to drive instructional decisions.

Contexts for Professional Growth

The activities of a strong professional development program for teachers implementing CMP emphasize four areas.

- experiencing
- planning
- teaching
- reflecting

Experiencing

First and foremost, to implement a problem-centered curriculum like CMP, teachers need deep understandings of the key mathematical ideas and ways of reasoning that are embedded in solving the problems within a unit. In addition, they need to see how understanding of these ideas develops over time and connects to content in other units. Thus, during the workshops (or whenever teachers are being introduced to a new unit), teachers should experience the curriculum in a way that is similar to what their students will experience. This does not mean they need as much time for each problem, nor that they must do every problem. Problems for the workshops should be chosen to highlight the development of key mathematical ideas. The supporting problems can be more quickly examined so that the flow of development is clear, but the main focus is on the key idea.

Professional development leaders should model good teaching; they should set a context for teacher learning, encourage teachers to investigate, and help teachers make their conclusions explicit. This allows teachers to focus on making sense of the mathematics needed to solve the problems posed. By setting the context as, *"How do you think your students might solve this problem?"*, the workshop leader can shift the focus to students' understanding. Teachers should be encouraged to make a good faith effort not to superimpose their own store of remembered knowledge on to each problem. The goal is not so much to find answers to the problem as it is to ask, *"What would my students bring to this problem? What solution strategies might they try? Which seem productive and rich in mathematical ideas? What are some of the misunderstandings that students might evince, and how can I best use discussions around these misunderstandings to help everyone learn more?"*

Some teachers may think that the problems, or the mathematical ideas, are too hard. A powerful strategy for helping teachers with the mathematics and showing what students can learn is to use examples of student work. This alleviates the anxiety of teachers who have never learned or understood the mathematics in the problem, or have no confidence in their ability to do the mathematics. It allows teachers to ask questions they might be reluctant to ask. In such an environment teachers can and do learn the mathematics of a unit. Positioning the mathematics and the teaching through the lens of the student helps provide a comfortable environment for discussions of teaching and learning of the mathematics.

Through follow-up discussions of the problems, the mathematical potential of the problems, the reasoning that students employ, and the connections that can be made become more explicit. Through such interactions teachers begin to value such questions as, *"What is the mathematics? At what stage are we in the development of understanding of the key idea? What do students need to bring to the problem? To what do these ideas connect in a student's future study of mathematics?"*

While effective teaching strategies are modeled and occasionally discussed during the study of a unit by the participants, it is most effective if attention to teaching becomes explicit in the professional development. Teachers will need help with the teaching model. Knowing how to launch a problem, how to assist and guide all students during the exploration, and how to summarize student understandings and strategies are very crucial to the development of the mathematics. A good stimulus for discussions on teaching is observation of good teaching, either live in a classroom or on video. Analyzing students' strategies can lead to conversations on how the classroom environment/discussion may have affected learning. This is also a time for teachers to experience collaborating to make sense of what evidence there is of good teaching. Developing the habit of asking, *"What aspects of the launch were effective? What aspects of the summary were effective? How would I address that student question?"* prepares teachers to make of themselves the same demands.

Planning

Planning is key to success with any problem-centered curriculum such as CMP. Professional development activities should include opportunities to plan collaboratively. Occasionally teachers should be asked to plan together to teach a problem, asking, *"What is the mathematics? What difficulties will students encounter? What mathematical discoveries might they make? How will I launch this?"* (See page 12.) It is crucial that administrators recognize that, while the planning load reduces somewhat after the initial implementation stage, there will always be a need for teachers to plan lessons and reflect on what students learned from the lessons, and for administrators to help find time for these planning and reflecting activities. This is a way to optimize and continue professional development.

For each class session it is important for teachers to identify the mathematical concepts or strategies, their stages of development, and the time needed to develop these understandings. The power of CMP does not lie in any one activity or any one unit. Important ideas are studied in depth within a unit and further developed and used in subsequent units. It is both the depth of understanding within units and the careful building and connecting of the units that allow students to develop to their fullest mathematical potential.

Initial planning can occur in the first summer, prior to the implementation of the CMP. However, teachers also need time during the year to plan, particularly with their colleagues. Planning sessions allow teachers to share problems they have experienced, learn new ideas from their colleagues, probe the mathematics more deeply, look for connections, and plan upcoming class sessions.

Once teachers are comfortable with the mathematics and inquiry-based instructional model, they are ready to look more closely at assessment and how to use assessment to evaluate students' knowledge and to inform their teaching. Fuller discussions on assessment are appropriate during the second year of teaching CMP and continued professional development. However, examining student work with a colleague is valuable. Asking questions about what the students' work shows not only deepens teachers' knowledge, but it can also serve as a guide to planning effective teaching strategies. Planning also allows teachers time to discuss and share management and grading strategies as well as ways to address the needs of diverse student populations.

Teaching

Teachers need to think critically about creating a classroom environment that fosters students' expectation that they will work together to solve problems, reason about possibilities, justify their ideas, and solutions, and look for connections. Posing problems that provide a challenge for the students, allowing students to explore the problem and guiding class discussion on the solution of the problems requires the teacher to play many roles at the same time.

Teachers need help in learning how to ask effective questions that can guide and probe students' understanding, and at the same time they need to learn to listen carefully to their students. These are not skills that teachers, even those with many years of experience, have traditionally practiced. District administrators who take the time to become knowledgeable about inquiry-based learning are better able to support teachers directly. They can help set the expectation that teachers will collaborate and learn from and with each other as the curriculum is enacted.

Setting and achieving high expectations for understanding, problem solving, representing, and communicating for all students is a task that confronts teachers on a daily basis. Reflecting on one's practice with a lens on student understanding is important for teachers to make progress. Establishing the kind of environment in a school where administrators support and expect teachers to collaborate with each other can change the whole school's daily focus to such teacher questions as, *"What evidence do I have that my students learned something? What did they learn?"*

Reflecting on Lessons

Professional development activities should model reflective practices. It is through reflection on their teaching and their students' understanding that teachers continue to grow in their capacity to build powerful mathematical experiences for all students. Planning with a colleague, peer coaching, observing a peer, or sharing with colleagues are some ways to encourage reflection.

Videotapes of lessons can serve as a catalyst for reflections. Caution must be exercised if videos are used. If a teacher within a building agrees to be video taped, then the focus should be students' learning rather than critique of the teacher. Centering conversations on student learning is a way to help the teacher think about his or her practice. *"What is there about my students' ways of approaching the problem that I like?" Why do I think this is effective? What should I do to encourage more of this? What aspects of my students' actions are not productive? Why is this? What can I do to redirect my students?"* Finding the fine line between trying to help the students be successful with the problem and allowing the students freedom to explore a more open problem will take reflection and growth over time.

Similarly, using rich collections of student work in professional development activities can focus teachers' attention on the role and importance of the summary phase of the lesson. When teachers study a collection of student work, some say that all of the solutions are acceptable, or they correct those that are not, and go on to the next lesson. But it is the analysis and comparison of the collection of student work that can bring the important mathematics to the forefront. Student work can also be the way to center discussions and reflections on students' understandings.

A variety of assessment tools can be used including mathematical reflections, quizzes, unit tests, projects, and district wide instruments. To be effective, discussions on student learning should go hand in hand with discussions on teaching. A focus on student learning leads naturally to looking at the development of ideas over time. Talking and planning with colleagues in different grade levels provides the opportunity for teachers to build and share a coherent curriculum vision. Collaboration and reflection are key elements in creating a community of teachers and administrators within the school that can support improvement in teaching and learning over time.

Teacher's Guides and Professional Development

The teacher materials that accompany each unit of CMP offer help with the same components that are included in a good professional development program. Part of the professional development should be to model how these materials might be used. But these materials should not be considered a replacement for the professional development necessary to get teachers started and for the district's support in keeping teachers enthused and learning after the initial implementation phase. Each unit contains:

- Help with the mathematics—an in-depth look at the mathematical ideas and how these are developed.

- Suggestions for planning effective launches, asking good questions, and leading powerful summaries.

- Suggestions for good assessments and how to manage them.

- Help in working with diverse or special needs populations.

- Connections to prior and future units and assistance in tracking where students should be in their development of key ideas.

If we believe it is a worthy goal to establish a safe and healthy environment in each classroom to enable students to learn together, then it becomes equally important that we acknowledge that teachers need time and opportunities to work with each other. No matter how informative the teacher support materials are, teachers will get more from them if they can plan or reflect with a colleague.

Encouraging teachers to share their successes is one way for schools and districts to promote teacher ownership of the curriculum. Sharing can be done within the school through mentoring new teachers or through shared planning times with other teachers, through district newsletters, through online discussion groups, or by volunteering to speak at local or state meetings. Networking, going to professional meetings, and joining mathematics teachers' association are all ways to continue to grow in mathematical knowledge and in pedagogical strategies.

Often overlooked is the problem of teacher turnover that occurs in virtually all middle schools. It is critical to develop a plan to provide professional development for new hires. It is equally important, and not simple, to develop collaborative relationships with experienced mathematics teachers. Such relationships are mutually beneficial to the new and experienced teachers, and in many instances result in lowering the rate of attrition of new teachers.

As teachers become comfortable with CMP, it becomes a natural part of the fabric of the school. A sense of complacency, a "We've done it!" feeling, sets in. This is a time for taking a more exacting look at the potential of the curriculum. These more advanced professional development experiences can re-energize teachers and result in improved student learning. Moving to this next level of implementation is a crucial step and one that is very often overlooked. Professional development is not a one-time nor a brief experience, but the essence of having teachers staying fresh, enthusiastic, and highly effective.

The Strength of Collaboration

It is through collaboration that progress is made and continued. It is through these collaborative professional exchanges of sharing ideas, planning, examining student work, looking for gaps, and finding ways to make even bigger gains in student understanding, reasoning, and communication that we continue to move forward. In the early stages of implementation, the community may include the entire staff of mathematics teachers, but as implementation continues, it is likely that teachers will rely heavily on their grade-level colleagues for support, ideas, and guidance. Professional development opportunities are needed to ensure that these collaborations are able to continue throughout the implementation, even after the curriculum appears to be institutionalized at the school.

Some issues that collaboration might focus on are: student understanding, perceived weaknesses as evidenced on local and state testing, teacher strategies, reports from teachers who have attended state or national conferences, preparing presentations for administrators or parents or state or national meetings, effective use of technology.

In Summary

Working as a community ahead of time to carefully select materials, become knowledgeable about the strengths of the materials and the reasons for the choice, examine the transitions points for students coming into CMP as well as the transition into high school, prepare the parents, administrators, school board members, and plan the implementation and professional development for teachers, will make a smooth and powerful implementation of CMP. All the constituent groups in the system are important in the education of children and, as such, need to be informed so that they can offer the most help possible to teachers and students.

Teaching CMP2

This section provides information about planning to teach CMP and suggestions for management. The discussion and suggestions come from our work with experienced CMP teachers. This material is intended to be read and used by teachers, so the text addresses teachers directly.

Connected Mathematics may be very different from curricula with which you are familiar. Because important concepts are embedded within problems rather than explicitly stated and demonstrated in the student text, you play a critical role in helping students develop appropriate understanding, strategies, and skills. It is your thoughtful engagement with the curriculum and your reflections on student learning that will create a productive classroom environment.

In planning to teach a unit, the first thing you need to do is become familiar with the content and the way the concepts, reasoning, and skills are developed. As you prepare, you will want to try to anticipate your students' learning and assess where difficulties might occur. The following section provides suggestions you can use as a guide as you plan to teach a unit.

Planning— Getting to Know a CMP Unit

The first stage in planning to teach a unit is becoming familiar with the key concepts and the way the unit develops concepts, reasoning, and skills. In general, the unit subtitle gives a broad view of the important ideas that will be developed in the unit. For example, the *Moving Straight Ahead* unit has the subtitle "Linear Relationships," which identifies linear relationships and functions as the central idea. What the title does not reveal are what aspects of linear relationships are developed and how understanding is enhanced. The following suggestions can serve as a guide for getting to know a unit at this more detailed level.

The Mathematical Ideas in a Unit

- In the Teacher's Guide, read the introductory material including the Goals of the Unit, Developing Students' Mathematical Habits, Overview, Mathematics Background and Content Connections to Other Units. These will give you a broad view of the mathematical goals and connections to prior and future units.

- Read the Summary of Investigations near the beginning of the Teacher's Guide and the Mathematical Reflections in the student books at the end of each Investigation. These outline the development of the mathematics in the unit.

- Look over the Assessment Resources for the Unit. They give you an idea of what students are expected to know at various points in the unit, and the level and type of understanding students are expected to develop.

The Development of the Ideas in a Unit

To help you investigate the details of concept and skill development and guide you as you teach each investigation, read the student unit and all of the problems and ACE questions. Then read the Mathematical and Problem-Solving Goals and the Summary of Problems that are given at the start of each Investigation. Ask yourself questions such as the following:

- *What part of the main mathematical goal of the unit is being developed? How does each problem in the Investigation contribute to the development of the mathematics? What level of sophistication do I expect my students to achieve in answering the problems in the Investigation?*

- *How will student responses show development in understanding the big ideas of the unit?*

- *What mathematical ideas will need emphasis?*

- *What connections can be made among the problems in this Investigation, to other Investigations in this unit, and to other units?*

- *How can I structure the writing assignment for the Mathematical Reflections so students get the most from it?*

- *What ACE questions are appropriate for my students to do after each problem?*

- *How long should this Investigation take?*

- *What can I do to assure the amount of time spent in class is appropriate for the problems and the goals of the Investigation?*

Guidance in answering these questions can be found throughout the Teacher's Guide in Pacing Charts, Assignment Guides, and sample answers for ACE exercises and Mathematical Reflections.

Teaching a Student Unit

The role of the teacher in a problem-centered curriculum is different from the curriculum in which the teacher explains ideas clearly and demonstrates procedures so students can quickly and accurately duplicate these procedures. A problem-centered curriculum such as *Connected Mathematics* is best suited to an inquiry model of instruction. As the teacher and students investigate a series of problems, it is through discussion of methods of solutions, embedded mathematics, and appropriate generalizations that students grow in their ability to become reflective learners. Teachers have a critical role to play in establishing the norms and expectations for discussion in the classroom and for orchestrating discourse on a daily basis. It is through the interactions in the classroom that students learn to recognize acceptable mathematical practices, and those needing explanations or justifications.

The CMP materials are designed in ways that help students and teachers build a different pattern of interaction in the classroom. The CMP materials are written to build a community of mutually supportive learners working together to make sense of the mathematics. This is done through the problems themselves, the justification students are asked to provide on a regular basis, student opportunities to discuss and write about their ideas, and the help provided to the teacher through the assessment package and the embedded problem-centered instructional model. In addition, the following are useful:

- To help teachers think about their teaching, the three-phase instructional model contains a *launch* of the problem, an *exploration* of the problem, and a *summary* of the problem. (See a detailed discussion of the instructional model for teaching CMP on pages 73–74).

- The teacher is provided with detailed help—Investigation by Investigation, and Problem by Problem. The Teacher's Guide contains a discussion of the Launch, Explore, and Summarize phases for each Problem. These discussions contain specific help on the focus for each Problem, how to build on previous Problem(s) or Investigation(s), what strategies or misconceptions students might have, and connections to other mathematical concepts. Also included are suggestions for specific questions to ask during each phase of instruction. Before you engage your class in a Problem, you will find it helpful to read the detailed teaching notes for it.

- The discussion on Organizing the Classroom (see page 101) contains helpful suggestions for organizing the classroom and encouraging student participation.

Reflecting as You Teach

The following questions are all part of teacher reflections on the effectiveness of the classroom environment:

- *Do the tasks engage the students, and are they effective in helping them learn mathematics?*

- *Do the activities stimulate the richness of discussion that helps students to develop mathematical power?*

- *Does classroom discussion encourage learner independence? Curiosity? Mathematical thinking? Confidence? Disposition to do mathematics?*

- *Does the classroom environment reach every student and support his or her mathematical development?*

- *What do my students know? What is the evidence? How does this shape what I plan for tomorrow?*

It is through reflection that teachers continue to grow and to develop the kind of classroom environment that encourages all students to become independent, confident, and reflective learners. The suggestions below are adapted from those submitted by CMP teachers:

Using Feedback From Class

In their Teacher's Guide or in a separate notebook, many teachers write brief notes or comments on important ideas or suggestions for what worked and what to do differently the next time they teach the unit.

- Use the classroom discussions, homework, or Mathematical Reflections as benchmarks for your students' understanding.

- Re-evaluate where you and your students are each day.

- Reflect on each student's understanding. What do you know about this student? Is this student participating in class discussions? Is he or she completing homework?

Finally, at the end of each day, each Investigation, or each unit ask yourself:

- *What evidence do I have of what my students learned?*

- *How should this affect my instructional decisions?*

Collaborating With Colleagues

Many teachers have found it valuable to plan with a colleague before, during, and after teaching the unit. Very often, student work is a focus for their discussions, as it provides a platform for discussing the mathematics in the Unit, Investigation, or Problem. Discussion can also cover effective teaching strategies and other issues related to teaching. The following sets of summary questions can be useful for working either alone or with colleagues. The Teacher's Guides also contain a wealth of information to help you plan your lessons.

A Quick Guide to Planning

GETTING TO KNOW THE UNIT

- It is important to understand the mathematics and how it is being developed. Read the Goals of the Unit, Mathematics of the Unit, and Content Connections to Other Units.

- Read the Mathematical Reflections in the Student Unit—they tell the story of the mathematics that is being developed in the unit.

- Look over the Assessment Resources.

- Work all of the Problems and ACE for each Investigation.

- Make use of the help provided in the student and teacher books for teaching.

- Use the Launch-Explore-Summarize (LES) as a guide for teaching each Problem.

- Keep notes on important ideas or suggestions for the next time you teach the unit.

- Use the Mathematical Reflections as benchmarks for your students' understanding.

- Reevaluate where you and your students are each day—teacher reflections are an important part in becoming a more effective teacher.

- Use the following questions as you plan to teach the Unit, each Investigation, or each Problem.

Questions to Think About
UNIT BY UNIT

- *What are the big mathematical ideas of this unit?*

- *What do I want students to know when this unit is finished?*

- *What mathematical vocabulary does this unit bring out?*

- *What might be conceptually difficult?*

- *What are important connections to other units?*

Questions to Think About
INVESTIGATION BY INVESTIGATION

- *What part of the mathematical goal is being developed?*

- *How does each Problem in the Investigation contribute to the development?*

- *What level of sophistication do I expect my students to achieve in answering the questions?*

- *Will their responses show the development in their understanding the goals of the unit?*

- *What ideas will need emphasis?*

- *What are the connections among the Problems, Investigations, and with other Units?*

- *How can I structure the writing assignment for the Mathematical Reflections to get the most from them?*

- *What ACE questions are appropriate for my students to do after the 1st problem, the 2nd problem, etc. in this Investigation?*

- *How long will this Investigation take?*

- *What can I do to assure the time spent in class matches the size of the problems and the goals of the Investigation?*

Questions to Think About
PROBLEM BY PROBLEM

Launch

- *How will I launch this Problem?*

- *What prior knowledge do my students need to call upon?*

- *What do the students need to know to understand the story and the challenge of the Problem?*

- *What advantages or difficulties can I foresee?*

- *How can I keep from giving away too much of the Problem?*

- *How can I make it personal to them?*

Explore

- *How will I organize the students to explore this Problem? (Individual? Pair? Group? Whole class?)*

- *What materials will students need?*

- *What are different strategies I anticipate them using?*

- *What kinds of questions can I ask:*
  - *—to prompt their thinking if the level of frustration is high?*
  - *—to make them probe further into the Problem if the initial question is "answered"?*
  - *—to encourage student-to-student conversation, thinking, learning, etc.?*

Summarize

- *How can I help the students make sense of and appreciate the variety of methods that may occur?*
- *How can I orchestrate the discussion so students summarize their thinking in the Problem?*
- *What mathematics and processes need to be drawn out?*
- *What needs to be emphasized?*
- *What ideas do not need closure at this time?*

- *What do we need to generalize?*
- *How can we go beyond? What new questions might arise?*
- *What will I do to follow-up, practice, or apply the ideas after the summary?*

Teacher's Reflections

At the end of each day, Investigation, or Unit, ask yourself:

- *What evidence do I have of what my students learned?*
- *How does this affect my instructional decisions?*

Finally, it is important to remember that "Rome was not built in one day." It takes time and patience to become the teachers we all aspire to be.

Classroom Environment

Organizing the Classroom

Helping students become independent learners is an important goal for *Connected Mathematics*. The Teacher's Guides point out opportunities for helping students reach this goal.

Classroom Setup

The way your classroom is set up can have a significant impact on learning. Here are some suggestions for creating an effective learning environment for students:

- Post the Mathematical and Problem-Solving Goals for the unit given in the Teacher's Guide and student books and check them off as the class meets them.

- Post a vocabulary list in the room so students know what words should be in their glossaries. Add words to the list for each unit as you proceed through the unit.

- Keep a list of assignments in the room for students who have missed class.

- Post upcoming assessments and due dates so students can anticipate your expectations

- Make tools (rulers, grid paper, angle rulers, and so on) accessible so students can decide which tools are appropriate for solving a problem.

- On the board, keep a list of unresolved questions for future discussion.

- Have textbooks, a mathematics dictionary, and other reference materials (almanacs, atlases, and so on) available for students to use.

- Have materials on hand that allow students to display their work and share their results with the class. Save student work for future reference by the class or for parent meetings. Record student work on overhead transparencies for class discussion and then make copies for absent students or save for future reference by the class.

Homework in CMP2

In *Connected Mathematics*, homework takes a role different from that in other curricula. Homework in *Connected Mathematics* is intended as an opportunity for students to think further about the ideas in a lesson. The lesson, rather than the homework assignment, is the primary unit of instruction, with homework as a vehicle for teachers to help students to process, practice, connect, and extend the ideas from the lesson. On a typical day in a *Connected Mathematics* classroom, far less time is spent assigning, doing and checking homework than may have been the case with other programs. The following sections contain some approaches *Connected Mathematics* teachers have taken in order to maximize the effectiveness of their time and students' time spent on homework.

Assigning Homework

You can use the Assignment Guide feature in the Teacher's Guide to help you assign homework. This feature appears on the At a Glance page for each Problem and indicates the ACE exercises which students should be able to answer after completing the Problem. The Assignment Guide for a Problem typically includes questions from each of the three ACE sections.

Teachers have generally found that the ACE exercises in *Connected Mathematics* are more substantial than the homework assigned in other curricula. So they often think differently about homework assignments. In particular, teachers begin to make more careful choices about which questions to assign and how to assign and grade them.

In general, the Assignment Guide in the Teacher's Guide for an Investigation will include all ACE exercises in that Investigation. In the spirit of *Connected Mathematics* materials, many more ACE exercises are provided than can reasonably be assigned as homework. However, this gives the teacher choices, so the materials can be tailored to the needs of a particular classroom of students. In addition, different communities have different expectations about homework, and classes meet for different lengths of time. These and other factors influence the pace and amount of homework assigned.

By answering the ACE exercises yourself before you assign them, you can anticipate difficulties and estimate the time it will take students to complete the assignment. Some teachers read and briefly discuss the ACE exercises in class before assigning them so that students understand what they are to do.

Students should attempt to answer all the assigned ACE exercises, but they may struggle with some. You might suggest that, if a student cannot solve a problem, he or she write a question about it, such as, *"What are 'increments of 5 campers'?"* or *"Which variable should go on the x-axis?"* Questions such as these focus the student on the area of difficulty, let you know the student's thoughts about the problem, and give you insight into the difficulty the student may be having. Some *Connected Mathematics* teachers begin class by allowing students to ask questions about the previous night's homework. The students are then given the opportunity to revise their work before turning it in.

Responding to and Grading Homework

How you respond to student work will depend on the reason you assigned the work. *Connected Mathematics* teachers have listed, among many others, the following reasons for assigning homework:

- To provide additional explanation and practice of the key mathematical ideas in the lesson

- To grade students' work

- To assess what students do and do not know in order to plan instruction

- To connect learning experiences on two consecutive days

- To instill good study habits

- To accomplish more mathematical study outside the time limits of the classroom

Because ACE exercises are rich, they may elicit a variety of answers and strategies from students. Dealing with this variety of responses can be time-consuming for teachers. Many *Connected Mathematics* teachers adapt how they respond to student homework based on the reason for a particular assignment. Clearly, if an assignment is given to assess understanding to plan instruction, the work will need more careful

attention from the teacher than if it is assigned to instill good study habits.

Some methods used by *Connected Mathematics* teachers to respond to students' homework are listed here.

- Prepare an answer key that covers the main elements of each exercise. (Detailed answers for all Problems and ACE exercises are in the Teacher's Guides.) Assign points to each Problem, and have students correct their work and total the points for correct answers.

- Write the exercise numbers for the previous night's assignment on the board. As students come into class, have them make a checkmark next to the numbers for which they have questions. Discuss only those problems.

- Choose a few exercises to read carefully and grade; discuss the rest in class.

- Go over the answers in class and have students check and revise their work. Then, each Friday choose a small set of exercises from the week's homework for students to turn in (this is sometimes referred to as a "homework quiz") for a grade.

- Collect the homework papers and check each exercise.

- To prevent losing some class time each day while checking homework, assign a few exercises over the course of the week and grade them all on one day.

- Assign a set of exercises at the beginning of the Investigation, informing students which of these exercises they should attempt each day. Spend a few minutes each day taking student questions about the previous night's work. Collect all of the exercises at the end of the Investigation.

- Give complete credit for satisfactory completion of the assignment. Give partial credit, as warranted, based on the number of exercises completed satisfactorily.

CMP Student Notebooks

It is helpful for students to keep their work in an organized notebook. The notebook can include notes, vocabulary, solutions to investigation problems, homework, and responses to mathematical reflections. By reviewing your students' notebooks, you can get a clearer picture of their mathematical development.

Because the *Connected Mathematics* units are three-hole punched, students can keep their books, along with their important work, in a three-ring binder. The binder can easily be divided into sections for a journal or notes, homework, vocabulary lists, quizzes, and tests. The binder can include work and notes written on loose-leaf paper or in spiral notebooks, which can be removed when the teacher wants to check some part of the notebook.

Some teachers have students designate a section of the notebook as a *journal*. In their journals, students record solutions to the Investigation problems, responses to Mathematical Reflections, and respond to queries generated by the class discussion, the teacher, or other students. Journals should be seen as an aid for students as they try out their thinking and develop complete responses and thoughtful conjectures.

Some teachers combine the journal and notes. Students record all journal entries on the left-hand side and the notes on the right-hand side. With this arrangement, students and teachers can separate the experimentation ideas from the summary of classroom ideas.

The following example shows the notebook guidelines one *Connected Mathematics* teacher gave to her students.

Example of a Notebook Organization[1]

Section 1: FORMS

In this section, keep assignment sheets, participation logs, and classroom rules and procedures.

Section 2: JOURNAL

This section should include:

- Any and all work you do for in-class problems; this includes your work on Investigation Problems and follow-ups and any handouts. Include words, charts, pictures, or anything else to show your thinking.

- Any notes you take; write anything that will help you remember your thinking. You should also record notes about the class summary of the ideas in each Investigation. These notes are for your reference as you solve in-class problems, answer homework questions, work on quizzes, and prepare for tests.

- Your Mathematical Reflections from each Investigation.

Section 3: VOCABULARY

In this section, you will create mathematical descriptions with examples of words you need to know. Use lined loose-leaf notebook paper for this section.

Section 4: HOMEWORK ASSIGNMENTS

This section should include your work on the ACE assignments. Your homework should be written on lined loose-leaf notebook paper or graph paper and clearly identified.

Section 5: ASSESSMENT

This section will include all check-ups, partner quizzes, tests, projects, and self-assessment.

Section 6: YOUR BOOK

Keep your unit inside your binder at all times. Please do the following to help you organize your work and to make it easier for me to review your notebook:

1. Date every entry and identify problems with problem numbers and the unit name.

2. Always revise what you have written by crossing it out, rather than by erasing. This saves you time and helps me to follow your thinking. It does not count against you to cross out your old work.

I will check your notebooks at unannounced times, and homework grades will be given.

After you complete a unit, clean out all the sections of your notebook except the "Forms" and "Vocabulary" sections. I will file your work for future reference and portfolio selections.

---

[1] These suggestions are adapted from Jan Palkowski, a middle school teacher in Traverse City, Michigan.
This teacher also has the students keep daily logs of their participation in classroom activities and dialogue.

It is recommended that you check notebooks often during the first few weeks of the semester. It is important to give students feedback early to make sure notebooks are being used correctly and to address any problems. Many teachers walk around the room while students are working and give comments or suggestions on maintaining notebooks.

Since keeping notes in mathematics class is new for many students, it is helpful to keep models of outstanding notes. This helps students understand your expectations. You can photocopy good examples to share with students. It might be helpful to have students evaluate their notes, journal entries, or vocabulary according to the models. At the end of the year, ask a student if you may keep his or her notes for the next year to have a complete example of how a notebook should look.

The Notebook Checklist can be used to evaluate students' notes periodically throughout a unit or at the end of a unit. In the Homework Assignments, list the items you would like to assess. Having students assess their notebooks before turning them in allows them to critically review their entries and organization.

Many teachers grade the journal, notes, or vocabulary sections of students' notebooks as well as the overall organization. Rubrics lend themselves nicely to the grading of notebooks, as you are generally looking for the completeness of ideas, notes, and vocabulary descriptions and records of the discussions from class. Some teachers give "Credit," "Partial Credit," or "No Credit" as a grade for notebooks.

There are a variety of methods for checking student notebooks. Here are some ideas you might try:

- Read and respond to a few students' journal entries each day.

- Collect papers from students at the end of each Investigation. Grade or respond to student work and then return the papers for students to replace in their notebooks.

- Collect notes at the end of a unit and grade them.

- Spot-check notebooks while students work on an assessment resource.

- Check notebooks at random.

- Give notebook quizzes. That is, periodically have students copy information from their notes on a sheet of paper; then grade just that information. (For example, *What were the three strategies we discussed for solving Problem 3.1? What was the answer to Problem 3.3 Part B?*)

Vocabulary

Vocabulary lists appear near the front of each Teacher's Guide. These lists are generally divided into three categories:

1. Essential terms developed in the unit
2. Terms developed in previous units
3. Useful terms developed in the unit

These lists indicate the mathematical terms developed in the unit. Based on your students' or school's needs, you may add to the lists or shift words from the useful to the essential column. You may choose to hand out the list of vocabulary terms from the Teacher's Guide when you begin the unit, or you may prefer to have students generate their own list as they encounter the terms in the unit.

Although there is a glossary in the back of each student book, we suggest that you have your students develop their own lists of definitions and examples. For important mathematical vocabulary, students need to have descriptions that carry meaning at their level of verbal sophistication. Encourage students to view their lists as working glossaries that they can add to and refine as they gain new insight and encounter new examples. Revising and updating descriptions can help students improve their working knowledge of the vocabulary. You might find it helpful to have students occasionally work in a group or as a whole class to discuss the various descriptions they have written.

The vocabulary lists and the definitions students generate can become quite involved and personal. Many students like to keep their lists from each unit to use as reference tools in later units. In some schools, students are required to save the lists they generate during the year to use the following year. This helps them make sense of new ideas by giving them previous references on which to build. Some schools give extra credit to students who begin the year with their vocabulary from the previous year.

To keep the vocabulary section organized, students are directed by some teachers to begin the school year with 26 sheets of paper in the vocabulary section of their notebooks. Each piece of paper is then labeled with a different letter of the alphabet. Students write the words, descriptions, and examples under the appropriate letter. Although the words are not in alphabetical order on the page, there is enough organization for students to locate specific words.

Pacing

When using *Connected Mathematics,* teachers should try to maintain a steady pace that will allow them to get through as much of the material as possible. Because ideas are developed over several problems, it is important for teachers not to spend too much time on any one problem. In some districts, district coordinators set timeline schedules to help teachers establish a sense of pacing. Each unit contains pacing schedules for 50-minute periods and block scheduling that were based on field testing. Depending on your district needs and schedule, it should be possible to do 6 to 8 units for each grade.

In the first year of implementation, some teachers may feel the need to supplement the materials with drill and practice. This will take time away from *Connected Mathematics* and slow the pace. Over time, teachers will learn the curriculum and understand that drill is incorporated into the lessons.

Although the primary focus of professional development is on the mathematics and pedagogy, teachers who are new to *Connected Mathematics* often have concerns about pacing, homework, grading, basic skills, and collaborative learning. These concerns may affect how a teacher sets the pacing of a unit. These issues should be addressed during professional development.

Absenteeism

Being absent in a CMP class is different from being absent in a traditional class. For example, students miss the experience of developing their understanding by working on a Problem and discussing key concepts and strategies. In *Connected Mathematics,* key concepts and skills are developed over several classroom

Investigations. If students are absent for only a day or two, they have not missed the entire discussion on a key idea. The following suggestions come from CMP teachers.

When Students Are Absent

- Keep assignments and activities posted in the classroom so students know what they missed.

- Have group members collect any materials that are passed out for absent group members.

- Establish note-taking buddies so students have someone to provide the notes.

- Keep a master copy of the classroom notes for students' reference.

- Have group or class members summarize what was done the previous day.

When Teachers Are Absent

Many teachers have found that, without some professional development, it is difficult for a substitute teacher to teach a Problem or lesson. Suggestions of activities that can be done when a substitute teaches the class are given here.

- **Partner Quizzes** Pairs can work on quizzes fairly independently, using their notes and books as resources. When it is possible, assigning partners the day before can reduce confusion as the class begins.

- **Review** Compile worksheets, using the additional practice problems from the units you have completed. If you teach seventh or eighth grade, you can use the problems from previous years.

- **ACE Exercises** Assign a set of ACE exercises to be done in class. You can provide incentives for students. For example, if work is done diligently the first part of the period, you might allow students to work with a partner for the second half of the period.

Note that all three suggestions work well if the teacher knows in advance that he or she will be absent. The last two suggestions also work for unexpected absences.

Student Configurations and Classroom Participation

Connected Mathematics provides opportunities for students to tackle mathematical problems individually, in pairs, in small groups, and as a whole class. Each of these arrangements of students enhances learning. The way you group your students will depend on the size, nature, and difficulty of the task. For a particular Problem, students might do individual work as part of the Launch phase or the launch may be a whole-class discussion. In the Explore phase, students may work individually, in pairs, or in small groups. They may take part in a whole-class discussion of a problem during the Summarize phase. The rationale for each of these grouping decisions is the nature of the problem and the goals of the lesson. The Teacher's Guide for each unit offers specific suggestions for grouping.

Whole-Class Work

The Launch of a CMP lesson is typically done as a whole class, yet during this launch phase of instruction, students are sometimes asked to think about a question individually before discussing their ideas as a whole class.

However, it is during the Summarize phase, when individuals and groups share their results, that substantive whole-class discussion most often occurs. Led by the teacher's questions, the students investigate ideas and strategies and discuss their thoughts. Whole-class discussion allows a variety of ideas to be presented and the mathematical validity of solutions to be tested. Questioning by other students and the teacher challenges students' ideas, allowing important concepts to be developed more fully. Working together, the students synthesize information, look for generalities, and extract the strategies and skills involved in solving the Problem. Since the goal of the summarize phase is to make the mathematics in the problem more explicit, teachers often pose, toward the end of the summary, a quick problem or two to be done individually as a check on how the students are progressing. Moving flexibly between whole-class

and individual work keeps the whole class focused, but allows each student to test his or her understanding of the ideas being discussed.

Individual Work

The teacher's notes often suggest that students spend some time working on a question individually before working with their partner or group. Asking students to first think about and try a question on their own gives them time to sort out their own ideas and assess what makes sense to them and what causes them difficulty.

For an occasional question, it is suggested that students work entirely on their own. Such questions may be less demanding than questions for which group work is suggested, or they may provide an opportunity for teachers to assess each student's understanding or skill at an important stage in the development of key mathematical ideas in the unit.

The ACE exercises at the end of an Investigation are intended to be solved individually, outside of class. These exercises give students a chance to practice and make sense of ideas developed in class. These exercises are narrower in scope and demand than are the Problems in the Investigations.

Pairs and Small-Group Work

Working collaboratively allows students to tackle more complicated and more conceptually difficult problems. Carefully managed, collaborative learning can be a powerful tool for teachers to use during classroom instruction. *Connected Mathematics* suggests two types of collaborative-learning groupings: partner work and small-group work.

Many of the problems in *Connected Mathematics* are mathematically demanding, requiring students to gather data, consider ideas, look for patterns, make conjectures, and use problem-solving strategies to reach a solution. For this reason, the Teacher's Guide often suggests that students work on the exploration of a problem collaboratively. Group work supports the generation of a variety of ideas and strategies to be discussed and considered, and it enhances the perseverance of students in tackling more complicated multi-step and multipart problems.

It is appropriate to ask students to think about a problem individually before moving into groups, allowing them to formulate their own ideas and questions to bring to the group. These multiple perspectives often lead to interesting and diverse strategies for solving a problem.

Group work is also suggested for some of the Unit Projects. These projects tend to be large, complicated tasks. Working in a group allows students to consider a variety of ideas and helps them complete the task in a reasonable amount of time.

You will want to determine group configurations in an efficient manner so class time is not wasted. You may find it easiest to decide before class how students will be grouped. There are various methods you can use to establish groups, such as assigning students to a group for a whole unit of study or randomly drawing for group assignments on a more frequent basis. You might also want to arrange the seating in the room to minimize movement during the transition from individual to group to whole-class settings.

Guidelines for Working in Pairs or Small Groups

It is important that you clearly communicate your expectations about group work to your students and then hold them to those expectations. You may want to hand out or post a set of guidelines so students understand their responsibilities. Below is a suggested set of guidelines.

Student Guidelines for Group Work

- Move into your groups quickly and get right to work.

- Read the instructions aloud or recap what the teacher has challenged you to find out. Be sure every group member knows what the challenge is.

- Part of group work is learning to listen to each other. Don't interrupt your classmates. Make sure each person's ideas are heard and that the group answers each person's questions.

- If you are confused, ask your group to explain. If no one in the group can answer the question, and it is an important question, raise your hand for the teacher.

- If someone in your group uses a word or an idea you do not understand, ask for an explanation. You are responsible for learning all you can from your group. You are also responsible for contributing to the work of your group. Your attempts to explain to others will help you to understand even better.

- Give everyone in the group a chance to talk about his or her ideas. Talking out loud about your thinking will help you learn to express your arguments and clarify your ideas.

- If your group gets stuck, go over what the problem is asking and what you know so far. If this does not give you a new idea, raise your hand for the teacher.

- Be prepared to share your group's ideas, solutions, and strategies and to explain why you think you are correct. Make sure you look back at the original problem and check that your solutions make sense.

- You are responsible for recording your group's ideas and solutions in your notes.

Suggestions for Encouraging Participation

When students work in groups, there is always a possibility that some students will dominate, while others will not participate. Making sure the size of the group is appropriate for the size of the task can help ensure that all students play a role. You can also facilitate participation by requiring that each group member be given the opportunity to share his or her thoughts and ideas before the group discussion begins. It is also helpful to give students some time to think about or work on the Problem individually before discussing it with their groups.

In the Summarize phase of instruction, groups share their findings with the class. It is important that all students have an opportunity to participate in this phase. To make sure all group members are prepared, you can randomly choose the presenter from each group or employ questioning techniques that involve all group members. Teachers have found these strategies to be useful:

- Have students assign numbers to each student in their group. Then, have them roll a number cube or draw to determine who will present the group's findings.

- Write each student's name on a craft stick, store the sticks in a cup at the front of the room, and choose one stick at random to determine who will present.

- Have the students choose the presenter for their group, but ask each of the other students a question related to the work.

The classroom conversation that occurs during the Summarize phase provides an important opportunity to push students' mathematical thinking. By examining and testing ideas, students can learn mathematical skills and strategies and make connections and generalizations. You might use the following suggestions to increase interaction and participation.

- Encourage students to respond to another group's or student's presentation, conjectures, strategies, or questions.

- Have students summarize the essence of a group's or student's presentation.

- After a group or student presents, have others in the class ask questions to challenge the group's or student's thinking.

- Ask a student to create and post an incorrect solution to stimulate the thinking of the class and generate a conversation.

- If you have a student who struggles, find opportunities for him or her to present when you know he or she has a correct answer.

- If there is repetition among strategies, have students discuss the similarities or contribute new thoughts, rather than just repeat ideas.

- Encourage students to look for common ideas in their strategies and representations.

Evaluating Student Learning

Grading in CMP2

The multidimensional assessment in *Connected Mathematics* provides opportunities to collect broad and rich information about students' knowledge. Teachers face the challenge of converting some of this information into a grade to communicate a level of achievement to both students and parents.

The following assessment items offer teachers an opportunity to assign grades: ACE exercises, Check-Ups, Quizzes, Mathematical Reflections, Looking Back and Looking Ahead (Unit Reviews) Unit Tests, Projects, notebooks, and Self-Assessments. The use of these assessments for grading and the value assigned to them vary from teacher to teacher. While most teachers view the problems as the time to learn and practice mathematical concepts and skills, some teachers will occasionally assign a grade to a problem. Some teachers also choose to grade class participation.

Two teachers' grading schemes for their CMP mathematics classes follow. These are given as examples of possible grading schemes. Note that each of these teachers has made independent decisions about how best to use the assessment tools in CMP for grading purposes.

Example 1: Ms. Jones' Grading System

I try to take several things into account when grading students in mathematics class. I work to build a learning community where everyone feels free to voice his or her thoughts so that we can make sense of the mathematics together. I try very hard to assess and grade only those things that we value in the classroom.

Participation

Because participating in discussions and activities is so important in helping the students make sense of the mathematics, this is one part of the students' grades. They rate themselves at the end of each week on how well they participated throughout the week. Below is a sample of the grading sheet they fill out. **The participation grade counts as 15% of their total mathematics grade.**

Participation Grading Sheet   Name _____

Week of _____

We have completed almost a full week of math class. Think about how well you participated in class this week.

1. Answer the following questions, as they will help you give yourself a fair participation grade for this week.

   ❑ Did you participate in the discussions?

   ❑ Did you come prepared to class, having done your homework, so that you could ask questions?

   ❑ Did you ask questions when you didn't understand?

   ❑ Did you LISTEN carefully to others?

2. Now count your "yes" responses.

   If you answered "yes" to ALL of them, HOORAY for you! You are doing a great job. Give yourself a **5**.

   If you answered "yes" to most of them, give yourself a **4**.

   If you answered "yes" to a couple of them, give yourself a **3**.

   If you answered "no" to several of these, give yourself a **2**, and rethink your role in this class or talk to your teacher.

3. I grade myself a _____ for this week.   Signature _____

Journal

Ideas become clear when we talk about them and when we write about them. Because I feel it is very important to be able to communicate mathematically in writing, students' journals also figure into their grade. We use the journals for problem solving, communicating what they do and do not understand, and reflecting on each Investigation to summarize the ideas. I try to collect them at least once every two weeks so I remain in constant communication with each student. **The journal grade counts as 15% of their total grade.** I use the rubric shown at the bottom of the page to grade journals.

Homework

The curriculum is problem centered. This means that the students will investigate mathematical ideas within the context of a realistic problem, as opposed to looking only at numbers. Students spend much of each class period working with a partner or in a small group trying to make sense of a problem. We then summarize the investigation with a whole class discussion. The ACE exercises assigned offer students an opportunity to practice those ideas alone and to think about them in more depth. Homework assignments are very important! They provide students the opportunity to assess their own understanding. They then can bring their insight and/or questions with them to class the next day. We usually start each class period going over the exercises that caused difficulty or that students just wanted to discuss. Keeping up with the homework (given about 3 or 4 times a week) helps students to stay on top of their learning. It also allows me to see what students are struggling with and making sense of. **Homework assignment grades count as 20% of their total grade.**

Partner Quizzes

All of the quizzes from CMP are done with a partner. Because a lot of what we do in class is done with others, I want to assess students "putting their heads together," as well. Again, I try to grade what I value, which is working together. **Quiz grades count as 20% of their total grade.**

Final Assessment

At the end of each unit an individual assessment is given. Sometimes it is a written test, sometimes a project, and sometimes a writing assignment. These serve as an opportunity for students to show what they, as individuals, have learned from the whole unit. **Test/project grades count as 30% of their total grade,** as they are a culmination of the whole unit.

Grading Summary:

- Participation **15%**
- Journals **15%**
- Homework **20%**
- Partner Quizzes **20%**
- Tests/Projects **30%**

Journal Grading Sheet

You will earn a 5, if:

- You effectively communicate your thoughts.
- You use appropriate vocabulary.
- You use a variety of strategies to solve problems.
- You write as if you are talking about mathematics.
- Your journal is well organized, and entries are labeled and dated.

You will earn a 4, if:

- You are effective in communicating your thoughts most of the time.
- You use some appropriate vocabulary.
- You use some different strategies when solving problems.
- Your journal is fairly well organized, and most entries are labeled and dated.

You will earn a 3, if:

- You attempt to communicate your thoughts but your entries are hard to follow at times; be sure to write ALL that you know.
- You use some appropriate vocabulary but need to use more.
- You need to work on using a variety of strategies to solve problems.
- Your journal is not organized with the entries labeled and dated.

If you earn a 2:

- Please see me.

Date Graded	Grade Received
_____	_____
_____	_____
_____	_____

Example 2: Mr. Smith's Grading Scheme

Journals (Part of the Notebook)

Collect student journals once a week.

Scoring Rubric for JOURNALS

5 Work for all Investigation problems (done in class, to date) and Reflections (well labeled and easy to find/follow)

4 Most class work and Reflections (well labeled and easy to find/follow)

3 Some missing class work or Reflections (not well labeled or easy to find/follow)

Below a 3 is not acceptable. Students have to come in at lunch or after school and meet with me and work on their journal until it is at least level 3.

Participation

Participation means questioning, listening, and offering ideas. Students are given a participation grading sheet every Monday, to be handed in on Friday. Students fill these out throughout the week, giving evidence of their participation in the class. On the sheets they are to note when and how they contribute to class discussion and when they use an idea from class discussion to revise their work or their thinking.

Scoring Rubric for PARTICIPATION

5 Student has made an extra effort to participate and help others in the class to understand the mathematics. Student gave evidence of participating all 5 days of the week.

4 Student made an effort to participate, giving evidence of at least 4 days of participation for the week.

3 Student made some effort to participate, giving evidence of at least 3 days of class participation for the week.

Below a 3 is not acceptable. I talk with student about his or her lack of effort. If no improvement is seen in the next week, a parent or guardian is called and informed of the problem.

Homework (selected ACE exercises)

In class, before homework is checked or collected, students are given the opportunity to ask questions about the assignment. I do not give answers or tell how to solve the exercise but, with the class's help, work with students to help them understand what the exercise is asking. Students have the right to revise any of their work while this conversation is

going on and not be marked down. Grading is strict on this work because students have the opportunity to take care of it themselves and get help.

Scoring Rubric for HOMEWORK

✔+ Close to perfect

✔ All problems attempted, most work done correctly

✔– Most problems attempted, some given answers wrong or incomplete

✔–– Not much work, most work wrong or incomplete

0 No work

Projects

A 6-point holistic rubric is used for all projects.

Scoring Rubric for PROJECTS

5 Project is complete, mathematics is correct, work is neat and easy to follow.

4 Project is mostly complete, most of the mathematics is correct, work is neat and easy enough to follow.

3 Project has some missing pieces, some of the mathematics is correct, work takes some effort by the teacher to follow.

2 Project is missing some major parts, there are several problems with the mathematics, it takes extra effort for the teacher to follow the work.

1 Project shows little to no significant work.

0 No project is submitted.

Check-Ups, Partner Quizzes, and Unit Tests

With partner quizzes, only the revised paper (the one turned in the second time) is scored for a grade.

Scoring Rubric for Check-Ups, Partner Quizzes, and Unit Tests

Each assessment has its own point-marking scheme devised by me. Points are determined by the amount of work asked for to solve each problem. Not all problems are awarded the same number of points.

Assigning grades to numbers and checks

5's and ✔+ = **A**
4's and ✔ = **B**
3's and ✔– = **C**
2's and ✔–– = **D**
1's and 0's = **E**

Comments on Partner Quizzes

The quizzes provided in the *Connected Mathematics* assessment package are a feature unique to the curriculum. The assumptions under which the quizzes were created present a unique management and grading situation for teachers.

- Students work in pairs.
- Students are permitted to use their notebooks, calculators, and any other appropriate materials.
- Pairs submit a draft of the quiz for teacher input, revise their work, and turn in the finished product for assessment.

Partner quizzes are designed to be completed by students working in pairs. There are several ways to choose student pairs for a quiz. Most teachers use one or more of the following:

- Students choose their own partners.
- Partners are chosen in some random way.
- The teacher picks the pairs to work together.
- Seating assignment determines partners.

Many teachers keep track of who works with whom and have a rule that you cannot have the same partner twice until you have been paired with everyone in the class at least once.

It is assumed that each pair of students will have one opportunity to revise their work on the quiz based on teacher feedback before submitting it for a grade. When a pair has completed the quiz, they can submit separate papers or one paper with both names on it.

Giving feedback generally involves telling students which questions they have answered incorrectly or how many of the possible points they would receive for a question. It should be seen as an opportunity to let students know if they are on track or if they need to rethink a problem. Giving feedback should not mean reteaching or leading students to the correct solution. Here are some methods *Connected Mathematics* teachers have used for giving feedback to students.

- Check the quizzes and write the number of points achieved next to each question. Then, allow the pair to revise all the questions.
- Check the quizzes and write the number of points achieved next to each question. Then, allow the pair to revise one question of their choice. (If they write in a different color, you need to check only the new information.)
- While students take the quiz, allow each pair to confer with you once about one problem.

Allowing students to revise their work is a new concept for many mathematics teachers. If you have never done this before, you might ask one of the language-arts teachers in your school how he or she orchestrates revision work for student writing, since this is a common practice in that discipline.

Quiz questions are richer and more challenging than Check-up questions. Many quiz questions are extensions of ideas students explored in class. These questions provide insight into how students apply the ideas from the unit to new situations. The nature of the partner quizzes provides a grading situation in which rubrics can assist in the evaluation of the students' knowledge. You may want to refer to the teacher suggestions, grading rubrics, and samples of student work in the Teacher's Guides.

Differentiated Instruction

This section contains specific suggestions of ways to present the *Connected Mathematics* curriculum to English language learners, to special needs students, and to gifted students.

In addition to the material presented here, please see the separate publication *Connected Mathematics 2 Special Needs Handbook for Teachers,* which contains many samples of ways to adapt CMP materials for special needs students.

English Language Learners

Mathematics and English Language Learners

English language learners (ELL) come into our classrooms from a variety of countries with a diverse set of experiences. They face the daunting tasks of adjusting to a new home and cultural environment, learning a new language, making new friends, and making sense of the rules, appropriate behaviors, and mechanics of a new school. Simultaneously, ELL students are experiencing many losses and trying to "fit in" with their new surroundings.

For teachers, working successfully with ELL students requires more than just teaching the content of courses. For language learners to achieve academic success, we must also support language goals and general learning strategies in the mathematics classroom (Richard-Amato & Snow, 2005). In addition, it is critical to create a friendly, supportive, and predictable classroom community. Some general suggestions are:

- Learn about your students' home countries, languages, and previous educational experiences.

- Value students' differences as resources.

- Stay connected to families.

- Clearly communicate school and classroom norms and expectations and be willing to check your assumptions at the door.

Teaching and learning with English language learners is a "lifelong process of learning, discovering, accepting, and trying" (Carger, 1997, p.45).

Classroom Environment and Teacher Talk

English language learners are often anxious about being in a classroom when they cannot speak English. Efforts to create a friendly environment that is respectful of students' diverse experiences and sets high expectations for learning will greatly support ELL students' opportunities for success. Part of establishing this kind of learning environment includes modifying the ways in which you talk with students. Patterns of speech,

intonation, or pace can often interfere with students' understanding of your expectations and therefore impact their abilities to engage in the mathematics lesson. Many of the suggestions below work for all students, including ELL students.

Classroom Community Create a classroom community that recognizes and values students' diverse backgrounds and experiences. Every child is born into a culture that socializes them to think in specific ways about many things we take for granted as common sense. When left unexamined, some cultural beliefs and practices can interfere with students' success in our classrooms. Find out who your students are, where they come from, and which languages they speak.

Expectations Keep expectations high and consistent. Provide effective feedback. Too often ELL students receive "feedback that relates to personality variables or the neatness of their work rather than to academic quality" (Jackson, 1993, p. 55). If we want our students to learn and improve their work and understanding, it is crucial to be specific, focus our comments on the academic components of students' work, and clearly communicate to students how to improve the overall quality of the work they do (Jackson, 1993).

Speak Slowly Slow down the rate at which you speak and simplify the language you use. Consider your intonation; avoid using slang, idioms, extraneous words, and long, complex sentences. Repeat key points. Rephrase to promote clarity and understanding. Summarize frequently. Use clear transition markers such as first, next, and in conclusion. Ask clear, succinct, high-level questions. (Carrasquillo & Rodriguez, 2002, Jameson, 1998)

Visual Communication Pair your instructional talk with visual communication cues such as pictures, graphs, objects, and gestures (Peregoy & Boyle, 1997).

Seating Up Front Seat students toward the middle or front of the classroom, in a place where you can observe them closely and where they can observe the classroom interactions of other students (Peregoy & Boyle, 1997).

Predictable Routine Even though your content will vary, follow a predictable routine and a stable schedule. Predictability in routine creates a sense of security for students who are experiencing a lot of change in their lives (Peregoy & Boyle, 1997).

Dictionaries Have dictionaries and other learning tools available and easily accessible to students.

Teaching Students the Norms of School

Students come from a variety of places and their constructs of school and purposes for education often greatly differ. We cannot expect that any of our students will tacitly understand the ways in which we "do" school. We must be explicit about our expectations. Problems between teachers and ELL students often occur because of language differences and unidentified assumptions about the social aspects of schooling. Therefore, it is important for teachers to help students learn what is expected of them in the school building and inside your classroom.

Create and consistently reinforce classroom norms to support students' understanding of what is expected socially and academically in the classroom.

Post homework assignments in a public place in the classrooms so students can be responsible for checking their assignments and keeping track of whether or not they submitted them.

Provide each student with a daily agenda. As a class, write the day's objectives, activities, and the homework assignment. Students keep these agendas in their notebooks for personal reference. It is also helpful to provide space on the agenda for students to check off the homework assignment once it has been completed and turned in. (See page 123 for an example of a daily agenda link.)

Pedagogical Strategies in the Mathematics Classroom

English language learners benefit from a variety of instructional strategies that lower their anxiety and help make content more comprehensible. Mathematical objectives should be cognitively demanding and grade appropriate. Language-related adjustments and modifications should be made, including how you modify your instructional delivery, but the cognitive demand of the mathematics should not be changed. The learning and teaching philosophy of *Connected Mathematics* support many, if not all, of the following strategies for ELL. These strategies are also just good teaching strategies to be used with all students.

Strategies Inherent in *Connected Mathematics*

Effective Questioning Use effective questioning techniques. Research highlights the fact that teachers "frequently use few higher order questions to all students, especially to those for whom they had low expectations" (Jackson, 1993, p. 55). Higher-order questions promote analytical and evaluative thinking, affirm students' self-perceptions as learners, and support students to think of themselves as knowledge producers rather than knowledge consumers (Jackson, 1993). (See pages 6–7 for a discussion of inquiry-based instruction.)

Cooperative Groups Use cooperative group work (see pages 106–108 for a discussion of cooperative group work). Research evidence demonstrates that cooperative group work can have a "strong positive impact on language and literacy development and on achievement in content areas" (Richard-Amato & Snow, 2005, p. 190).

Active Participation Create opportunities for students to participate with you, each other, and the mathematical content. Active participation provides students with opportunities to learn both mathematics and English. Encourage your students to ask questions of each other. (See pages 73–74 for a discussion of classroom interactions during the Launch–Explore–Summarize phases of a lesson.)

Brainstorming Use class brainstorms, predictions, quick writes, and outlines as ways to access students' prior knowledge. It is also helpful to write students' ideas on the chalkboard so they can see them written correctly in English.

Prior Knowledge Consider the context of the problem. Context is meant to support students' entry into a problem by connecting to their prior knowledge and preparing them for what lies ahead. If students are unfamiliar with names, places, or objects, it will be difficult for them to access the mathematics. Sometimes it is possible to change the context of a problem without affecting the mathematics of the problem or the objectives of the lesson. Incorporate names and places from students' home countries or situate actions within cultural practices with which students are familiar. This is also a great opportunity for students to learn common English words used in daily life. Include words in the math problems that students need to know and avoid using slang, idioms, or extraneous language. (See pages 6–7 for a discussion of context in a problem-centered curriculum.)

Expression of Ideas Provide many opportunities during class for students to explain and justify their ideas.

Journals Use journals and quick writes to provide students with opportunities to write in the mathematics classroom. Use the following suggestions as meaningful writing activities:

- Restate the problem in your own words.

- Explain how you solved the problem.

- How do you know your answer is right? (Richard-Amato & Snow, 2005)

- What do you know so far about …?

(See pages 102–103 for a discussion of student journals.)

Model Behaviors Model what you want your students to do. Students may not understand what you say, and actions will support their understanding. For example, use visual prompts such as hand movements, facial expressions, or other body movement that suggests meaning for a word or phrase.

Support Vocabulary Development

Highlight Mathematical Vocabulary Students must understand mathematical terminology and key words to gain access to any math problem. Isolate important vocabulary and phrases by circling or underlining them in the text.

Bilingual Vocabulary Chart Create and maintain a Word Cluster or Vocabulary Chart in the classroom and in students' notebooks where new terms and their definitions are written in both English and the student's first language. Pictures are also useful additions. (See page 121 for examples of graphic organizers and 104–105 for a discussion of the development of vocabulary in *Connected Mathematics*.)

Practice Out Loud Practice speaking hard-to-pronounce words verbally as a class. It is beneficial for students to practice reading and pronouncing words correctly.

(See page 122 for five guidelines for simplifying language.)

Graphic Organizers

Use graphic organizers to scaffold your learning activities and provide ELL students access to the mathematical content. (See page 121 for examples of graphic organizers.) Graphic organizers include:

- Venn diagrams
- concept webs
- timelines
- lists
- outlines
- tree diagrams
- charts

Reading, Writing, and Waiting

Time to Prepare Give students time to read silently before asking them to discuss their ideas with a small or large group. It is also recommended to provide time for students to write their ideas on paper before they share them publicly. This will give students time to sort through their ideas before they are asked to perform in front of teachers and peers.

Write and Speak Directions Post task directions on the overhead or chalkboard while you simultaneously read the directions and have students follow along. This affords ELL students the opportunity to read the English text silently while they hear it spoken correctly.

Write in English Encourage ELL students to write in English even if the spelling and grammar is incorrect. It is also helpful for students to use a combination of English and their first language when they write in their notebooks.

Give them Time Use extra wait time so ELL students will have an opportunity to hear the question, translate the work, understand its content, formulate a response, and then speak.

Assessment of English Language Learners

Students' lack of English proficiency will affect test performance when tests are given only in English. It is also necessary to consider how students' cultural backgrounds and previous experiences might affect their ability or willingness to participate in an assessment activity. "Because schooling practices tend to conform more or less to middle-class European-American experiences and values, students from other cultural backgrounds may be misassessed by virtue of cultural and other experiential differences." (Peregoy & Boyle, 1997, page 93) Therefore, your assessment practices should allow students to show what they know in a variety of ways.

Diversity When creating assessments, consider the diversity of students' cultural, linguistic and special needs (Peregoy & Boyle, 1997).

Variety Use a variety of assessments in a variety of formats including small-group work, individual activities, drawing pictures, creating posters, engaging in interviews, constructing portfolios, journal writing, projects, and self-assessment. (See pages 77–80 for a discussion of assessment in *Connected Mathematics*.)

Rubrics Be clear and consistent with your grading system and standards. Rubrics are an excellent tool for itemizing the criteria on which students will be assessed and helping students understand what you are looking for (Richard-Amato & Snow, 2005).

Working Together Peer editing is an opportunity for students to read, edit, and comment on each other's work while gaining reading and writing experience.

Time Allow sufficient time for all students to complete the assessment.

Fewer Exercises Consider the number of exercises you assign students for homework. It will take ELL students much longer to read and make sense of the exercises than native-English speakers. Often ELL students get so bogged down in the reading comprehension that they never get to the mathematics. It will be much more meaningful and productive for both you and the students if you assign 5 or 6 well-designed exercises (and they'll be more motivated to try them), rather than a page or two of 10 to 20 exercises.

Rebus Techniques

The following suggestions follow guidelines known as rebus techniques for English language learners. *Rebus* is a general term referring to the use of pictures or other visual images to represent words or symbols. Some of these techniques are similar to those in the preceding sections.

Original Rebus Technique

On a sheet of paper, students copy the text from all or part of a page before it is discussed. During discussion, students then generate their own rebuses for words they did not understand as the words are made comprehensible through pictures, objects, or demonstrations.

This strategy ensures that English learners benefit from written communications in the same way as their English-proficient peers. While written text summarizes key concepts, includes background information, and provides directions for completing tasks, English learners often do not benefit from such communication.

In the past, English learners have been traditionally paired with English-proficient students who are asked to read aloud written text. However, this approach does not provide English learners with access to written communication. For example, English learners are asked to rely on memory when trying to recall the written information—something not required of their peers. Furthermore, simply reading information aloud does not ensure that the words are made comprehensible to the English learner. Therefore, the Original Rebus technique offers a strategy that makes written communication meaningful to English learners, without depending on peer cooperation or memory.

1. Teachers identify text perceived to be difficult for English learners to comprehend. Examples of such text may be questions appearing in Mathematical Reflections, Applications, and Connections sections of the program.

2. English learners receive a copy of the rewritten text when the corresponding page is introduced to the class. As the information from the student book is read aloud, teachers make key words understandable. For example, a teacher may demonstrate the word "snapshot" by showing a photo of a pet.

3. After students comprehend the word, the teacher writes it on the board so English learners can connect the written word with a specific meaning. At this time, English learners create an original rebus over that key word on their sheet of paper. This rebus will then help the English learners recall the meaning of the word when referring back to the text during independent work.

Note: It is essential that English learners draw their own rebuses. This ensures that whatever symbol they choose to draw has meaning to them. The problem with providing professional or teacher-drawn rebuses is that simple drawings, by themselves, do not often convey a universal understanding of the words. For example, many English-proficient students were not able to correctly identify a rebus when the word below was covered, yet could do so when they were able to view both the word and rebus. This suggests that the written word, not the rebus, conveyed the meaning in such situations. Moreover, if English learners are required to create their own rebuses, they then choose which words need to be coded. Depending on the level of English proficiency, the number of coded words can vary greatly among students.

Diagram Code Technique

Students use a minimal number of words, drawings, diagrams, or symbols to respond to questions requiring writing. Learning to organize and express mathematical concepts in writing is a skill students develop over time. If English learners are not given this same opportunity, they miss an important component of the math curriculum. This strategy provides alternate ways for students not yet proficient in writing English to express mathematical thinking on paper. While their responses will not be in the same format as those of their English-proficient peers, English learners still have the same challenge: they must record and communicate mathematical ideas so that someone else can understand their thinking.

1. At the beginning of the program, teachers model and encourage English learners to use this approach when writing answers to questions presented in the program.

2. To introduce this approach, the teacher writes several questions requiring written responses on the board. These questions should be simple with obvious answers.

3. The teacher then shows the English learners how to answer each question without writing complete sentences and paragraphs. At the end of this session, the teacher should have modeled answering questions by using and/or combining minimal words, drawings, diagrams, or symbols.

Note: This approach can be used for any written response in the program, but it is especially useful for responding to questions found in Mathematical Reflections. Since this part of the program provides a vehicle for assessing how well students have understood key concepts of the unit, this approach enables teachers to evaluate their English learners' progress as well.

Chart Summary Technique

This technique involves presenting information by condensing it into a pictorial chart with minimal words. This extension of the Diagram Code technique offers English learners another way to organize and express mathematical thinking with a minimal amount of writing.

1. At the beginning of the program, the teacher shows various charts on any subject. The charts need to be simple, include pictures, and have a minimal number of words.

2. The teacher then creates and writes a question on the board that relates to each chart. For example, the teacher might show a chart of the life cycle of a plant divided into four sections. For this chart, the teacher could ask this question: What are the growth stages of a plant?

3. The teacher continues by showing how the chart answers this question by pointing to the drawings in each section, showing the seeds, roots, stem, and flower. The teacher also points out how each section has been labeled.

4. At the end of this session, English learners should be able to respond to a question by creating a chart with pictures and minimal words.

Note: This approach may be an alternative for English learners when responding to some of the Unit Projects requiring detailed writing.

Rebus Scenario Technique

Teachers make use of rebuses on the chalkboard during discussions and when presenting information. While modifications for primary mathematical concepts may be perceived as necessary for English learners, there may be a tendency to omit such techniques for "enrichment" information, such as text appearing under "Did You Know?" However, if programs offer English-proficient students such information, then English learners should also have an opportunity to acquire the same knowledge. Therefore, the Rebus Scenario offers teachers a simple way to ensure that all students have access to both the core and enrichment aspects of the *Connected Mathematics* program.

The teacher assesses what key words may not be understood by the English learners. As each of those words is presented, the teacher simultaneously draws a rebus on the board.

Note: If there are English-proficient "artists" in the classroom, teachers may opt to implement this approach in a slightly different way. Prior to the lesson, a teacher can ask an artistic student to come to the chalkboard to draw rebuses for targeted words. When using this approach, the teacher can then just point to the appropriate drawings during the lesson. If there is no time prior to a lesson, the artistic student can be asked to draw the rebuses as key words are presented. With this latter approach, it is important that the artist knows which words to represent as rebuses and to draw quickly.

Enactment Technique

Students act out mini-scenes and use props to make information accessible. This technique ensures that all students comprehend hypothetical scenarios presented throughout CMP. With this technique, English learners are not excluded from lessons involving situations reflective of real-life scenarios.

1. Teachers decide which simple props, if any, will enhance the enactment. These props are gathered prior to teaching the lesson.

2. At the time of the lesson, students are selected to assume the roles of characters mentioned in a CMP problem or scenario.

3. These students then pantomime and/or improvise speaking parts as they enact the written scenario presented in CMP.

Note: There may be a tendency to select only English-proficient students for mini-scene roles; however, many parts can also be given to English learners. For example, roles such as pantomiming shooting baskets or pretending to ride a bicycle can be easily enacted by English learners, as these kinds of parts do not require students to speak English.

Visual Enhancement Technique

The Visual Enhancement technique uses maps, photographs, pictures in books, and objects to make information understandable by providing nonverbal input. This technique is most helpful for conveying information that is unlikely to be understood through enactment or creating rebuses. When pictures or real objects are added to lessons, English learners have the opportunity to receive the same information presented to their English-proficient peers, who are able to understand the written text without visual aids. This approach ensures that English learners equally acquire and benefit from descriptive and/or background information sections of the program.

1. Teachers decide if information on a page is unlikely to be understood with a rebus or by having students create an enactment. For example, maps are often used with this technique to help students understand what part of the world an informative section or investigation is centered around. In contrast, a mere rebus "outline" of the same country would not be likely to be understood by anyone. Likewise, topics such as video games, different kinds of housing, and newspaper advertisements are more easily comprehended by merely showing examples than by trying to draw something representative of the topic.

2. When teachers decide visual aids are the best approach for making information accessible, examples are sought prior to teaching the lesson.

3. Teachers then show the visual aid at the appropriate time during the lesson.

Note: In the first year of implementation, English-proficient students can earn extra credit by finding appropriate visual aids for targeted lessons. Teachers can then keep the pictures, objects (if possible), and book names (with page number) on file for use in subsequent years.

Summary

The six techniques (Original Rebus, Diagram Code, Chart Summary, Rebus Scenario, Enactment, and Visual Enhancement) ensure that English learners will receive the same mathematics curriculum as their English-proficient peers. Although the techniques differ in implementation, they all offer ways for English learners to acquire and express the mathematical ideas presented in CMP.

Although these approaches have been created specifically for English learners, they can be equally effective for many special-education students.

SUMMARY OF REBUS TECHNIQUES

Original Rebus Technique On a sheet of paper, students copy the text from all or part of a page before it is discussed. During the discussion, students generate their own rebuses for words they did not understand. This technique offers a strategy that makes written communication meaningful to students with language difficulties. First the teacher identifies text which contains important ideas and may be difficult for students with language difficulties. As this part of the text is discussed, the teacher tries to make key words understandable through pictures, objects, or demonstrations. Students create their own pictorial rebus for each of the key words.

Diagram Code Technique Students use a minimal number of words, complemented by diagrams or drawings to organize and respond to questions. The teacher should introduce and demonstrate how to express mathematical thinking without having to write in complete sentences. The ultimate goal is, of course, to have students progress towards being able to communicate mathematical thinking in writing as well as in these diagram codes.

Chart Summary Technique This is an extension of the Diagram Code. The technique involves presenting information by condensing it into a pictorial chart. As before, the teacher must model this technique so students see what is expected.

Rebus Scenario Technique To make enrichment information available to English learners, the teacher supplies quickly drawn rebuses on the chalkboard for key words in material like a "Did You Know?" passage. An artistic student may also be asked to sketch key word rebuses.

Enactment Technique Students act out mini-scenes and use props to make information accessible. This technique ensures that all students comprehend hypothetical real-life scenarios presented throughout CMP.

Visual Enhancement Technique The teacher decides if information in the text is unlikely to be understood with a rebus, as above, and provides visual aids to make information accessible.

Examples of Classroom Materials

Graphic Organizers

Graphic organizers can be used by the teacher to present information or by the students to organize information and to compare and contrast concepts and ideas. Graphic organizers such as word clusters, rebuses, and vocabulary charts can be used to support vocabulary development. Venn diagrams, concept maps, and other techniques can help students organize information.

Word Clusters
Write mathematical terms on sentence strips and group them together to show how they are connected. Hang the sentence strips from the ceiling or on a wall for quick reference.

Addition +	Divide ÷	Multiply ×
Add	Dividend	Factor
Sum	Division	Product
Addend	Quotient	Mutiples
Plus		

Rebuses
Create rebus pictures or symbols for words the students need help to understand.

Add +	Subtract –	Triangle ▲

- Students can draw the symbols directly over the words.
- A sheet of these symbols can be kept in the vocabulary section of students' binders.

Vocabulary Charts
The use of word cognates (linguistically related words) help students connect words in English to words from their own language that are familiar. Not all words have cognates. However, all terms are put on this chart even if they don't have cognates.

Term	Description	Example	Cognate
Factor	One of two or more whole numbers that are multiplied to get a product.	2 x 3 = 6	Factor
Prime number	Number with only 2 factors, 1 and itself	**3** 1 x 3 **1** 1 x 7	Número Primo

Venn Diagrams
Use Venn diagrams as a way to compare and contrast information. The example below is from CMP2, *Data About Us*.

Similarities

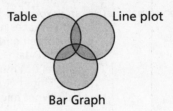

Table · Line plot · Bar Graph

Concept Maps
Concept maps are used to organize topics or categories and to visually represent connections between concepts and ideas.

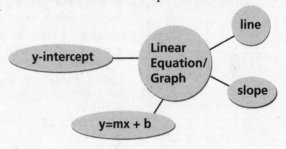

y-intercept · Linear Equation/Graph · line · slope · y=mx + b

Tree Diagrams/Hierarchy
Use tree diagrams to organize ideas from the general to the specific and to support understanding of the relationships between concepts.

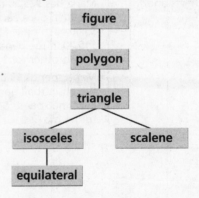

figure · polygon · triangle · isosceles · scalene · equilateral

Charts, Lists, and Timelines
Other ways to organize information include making charts, lists, and timelines.

Five Guidelines for Simplifying Language

Guideline	Original Text	Simplified Version
1. Use short sentences and eliminate extraneous material.	Samuel is getting a snack for himself and his little brother, Adam. There are two candy bars in the refrigerator. Samuel takes half of one candy bar for himself and half of the other candy bar for Adam. Adam complains that Samuel got more. Samuel says this isn't true, since he got half and Adam got half. What might be the problem?	Sam and Adam have two candy bars. Sam eats half of one candy bar. Sam gives Adam half of the other candy bar. Adam is mad. He thinks Sam has more candy. What is the problem?
2. Change pronouns to nouns.	Jorge made two graphs but he forgot to label them.	Jorge made two graphs. Jorge forgot to label the graphs.
3. Underline key points or vocabulary.	**Problem 1.1** **A.** How are the graphs alike? How are the graphs different? **B.** How can you use the graph to find the total number of letters in all of the names? **C.** Collect the data for your class and use graphs to represent the data distribution.	**Problem 1.1** **A.** How are the graphs <u>alike</u>? How are the graphs <u>different</u>? **B.** How can you use the graph to find the <u>total number of letters</u> in all of the names? **C.** Collect the <u>data</u> for your class and use <u>graphs</u> to <u>represent</u> the data distribution.
4. Turn narratives into lists.	Look back at the graphs that you have made in this unit. Find several graphs that show relationships in which y both increases and decreases as x increases. Describe each graph in words.	Look at the graphs you made. **A.** Find a graph where y increases and x increases. **B.** Find a graph where y decreases and x increases. **C.** Use words to describe each graph.
5. Use charts and diagrams.	Maria has $25.00 in the bank. She mows the lawn once each week and earns $5.00 each time. Suzanna only has $15.00 in the bank. She baby-sits her little brother for $2.00 each weekday. Maria spends $3.00 each week to go to the basketball game with her friends. Suzanna spends $4.00 each week to go to the movies.	<table><tr><td></td><td>**Bank**</td><td>**Earns**</td><td>**Spends**</td></tr><tr><td>**Maria**</td><td>$25.00</td><td>$5.00/wk</td><td>$3.00/wk</td></tr><tr><td>**Suzanna**</td><td>$15.00</td><td>$2.00/day</td><td>$4.00/wk</td></tr></table>

Daily Agenda • 6th Grade

Monday	Tuesday	Wednesday	Thursday	Friday
Objective: Activities: Homework:	Objective: Activities: Homework:	Objective: Activities: Homework:	Objective: Activities: Homework:	Objective: Activities: Homework:
Monday	**Tuesday**	**Wednesday**	**Thursday**	**Friday**
Objective: Activities: Homework:	Objective: Activities: Homework:	Objective: Activities: Homework:	Objective: Activities: Homework:	Objective: Activities: Homework:

Special Needs Students

Special Education Within CMP

Connected Mathematics can be and has been successfully implemented in classrooms that include special education students. We believe that *Connected Mathematics* provides all students, even those with special needs, with opportunities to engage in cooperative learning, to take leadership roles, and to enhance self-esteem and self-acceptance.

Making Accommodations

Some may claim CMP offers more of a challenge for special education students due to its language-based curriculum; however, many suggestions by researchers in the field of special education for assisting in making mathematics accessible to special needs students are already incorporated within the CMP curriculum. The CMP *Special Needs Handbook for Teachers* contains a wealth of samples of accommodated materials. Further accommodations will most likely still need to be made for special education students. Those accommodations should come from each students' Individual Education Program (IEP) and additional accommodations that you, as a teacher, feel are beneficial to the students you serve.

Please keep in mind that the guidelines in the *Special Needs Handbook* are suggestions. Not all suggestions are applicable for every student, nor will every suggestion work for all students. It is important to have good communication with your students' special education teacher and other providers, as well as his/her parents to enable that the maximum benefit from learning is being carried through.

Embedded Special Needs Strategies

The curriculum of the Connected Mathematics Project is already embedded with many of the strategies that researchers and practitioners indicate as beneficial to special education students. The conceptual framework upon which CMP is built involves sound teaching principles and practices for students, which is essentially the same foundation for working with special education students. To begin with, CMP was developed with the belief that calculators should be made available to students, which aligns with many accommodations that special education students are given in terms of calculator use. Furthermore, the CMP curriculum involves manipulatives. While it is stressed within the framework of CMP that manipulatives are to be used only when they can help students develop an understanding of mathematical ideas, it should be clear that special needs students may need to use the manipulatives to help develop their understanding more often than general education students.

CMP uses real-life problems, a pedagogical technique repeatedly stressed in reaching special education students in mathematics classrooms. An emphasis on significant connections which are meaningful to students, among various mathematical topics and between mathematics and problems in other disciplines, assisted in guiding the development of CMP. Maccini and Gagnon (2000) demonstrated that the embedding of problems within real world contexts improves the motivation, participation, and generalization for special education students.

Other practices that help to facilitate teaching mathematics to students with special needs already within the framework of the *Connected Mathematics Project* include: repetition and review, keeping expectations high, teaching conceptual knowledge, and cooperative or group activities. The student materials of CMP enable repetition and review. The ACE section at the end of every Investigation allows students to tackle additional exercises from the unit as well as to work on problems that are connected to earlier units. Furthermore, the end of each book includes a Looking Back and Looking Ahead section which summarizes through problems the learning students have completed in the particular Unit, and also connects it to earlier units.

The *Connected Mathematics Project* holds high expectations for its students—all of its students. This belief is reflected in the ideology and the overarching standard of the curriculum:

All students should be able to reason and communicate proficiently in mathematics. They should have knowledge of and skill in the use of the vocabulary, forms of representation, materials, tools, techniques, and intellectual methods of the discipline of mathematics. This knowledge should include the ability to define and solve problems with reason, insight, inventiveness, and technical proficiency.

CMP teaches conceptual knowledge and skill. As in the above definition, skill means not only proficiency, but also the ability to use mathematics to make sense of situations. CMP helps students to understand the methods, algorithms, and strategies they use.

Cooperative Learning Groups *Connected Mathematics* provides opportunities for students to work in small groups and pairs, as well as whole class, or individually. Research in the field suggests that cooperative groups can be beneficial to special education students; however, some attention should be paid to the groupings to ensure that students with special needs are able to actively participate. Merely placing a student within a group does not result in that student becoming a part of the group. While studies have shown that cooperative learning has positive benefits on students' motivation, self-esteem, cognitive development, and academic achievement, the very dynamic of these learning methods may exclude special education students due to their disparities in skills, such skills as content area, communication, and social skills (Brinton, Fujiki, & Montague, 2000). In discussing the structure of cooperative groups, researchers stress the importance of providing opportunities for children with special needs (or any diverse learners) to actively participate.

Examples of Classroom Materials

For each Investigation in CMP2, the *Special Needs Handbook* contains a sample modification of an ACE exercise. Taken together, these nearly 100 samples illustrate the wide variety of accommodation techniques that may be applied to individual students as needed.

ACE Accommodation

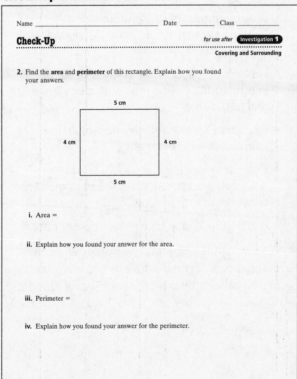

The *Special Needs Handbook* also contains a sample modification of one assessment tool for each CMP2 Unit.

Check-Up Modification

Gifted Students

Connected Mathematics is a curriculum developed to provide challenges appropriate for every student including the mathematically gifted child. The curriculum gives all students the opportunity to learn key mathematical concepts in depth and to make valuable connections that will benefit them in future mathematics classes.

Components of an Effective Program for Gifted Students

The National Council of Teachers of Mathematics made suggestions on how to provide opportunities for the mathematically gifted in the publication *Providing Opportunities for the Mathematically Gifted K-12* (NCTM, 1987). They proposed 16 essential components for programs for the mathematically gifted. A subset of these sixteen components, that directly relate to the mathematics curriculum are listed below. The program should:

- Contain good, high quality mathematics which is challenging, broad, and deep

- Nurture higher-order thinking processes and open-ended investigations

- Prompt students to communicate effectively by reading, writing, listening, speaking, and thinking mathematically

- Have problem solving as a major focus and include applications of mathematics to real situations

- Encourage students to experiment, explore, conjecture, and even guess

- Provide opportunities to use learning resources (texts, calculators and computers, concrete manipulatives)

- Relate mathematics to other content areas.

Connected Mathematics possesses all of the components described above, while maintaining a goal of mathematical proficiency for all students.

Modifications for Gifted Students

In order to provide a curriculum appropriate for gifted students, modifications in both the content and learning environment may be necessary. Maker and Nielson (1995) describe content and process modifications that should be made.

Modifications in Content:

- Students need a variety of problems to work.

- The content of the curriculum needs to be organized around key concepts or abstract ideas, rather some other organization (as noted by Bruner, 1960).

- Problems should be complex and students should be pushed to abstraction. (Additional opportunities for abstraction are described in Teacher's Guides of *Connected Mathematics*, particular in Going Further features described below.)

Modifications in Process:

- Promote higher levels of thinking by stressing *use* rather than *acquisition* of information. (Students continue to use information from previous units in the current unit they are studying in the *Connected Mathematics* series.)

- Provide open-ended questions in order to stimulate divergent thinking and to "contribute to the development of an interaction pattern in which learning, not the teacher, is focus" (see page 5).

- Teachers should guide student discovery of content and encourage questions of why and how things work. (*Connected Mathematics* Problems often ask students to think about the questions of why and how.)

- Students must be given opportunities to express their reasoning; (Students are constantly asked to explain or justify their reasoning in *Connected Mathematics*.)

- Group interaction should be a regular part of the curriculum for gifted students to enable them to develop social and leadership skills.

Connected Mathematics is designed so that many of the modifications described by Maker and Nielson are embedded in the curriculum. Other simple modifications are possible in order support gifted students and still maintain the integrity of the curriculum.

Other Modifications Renzoulli and Reis (2003) discuss the Schoolwide Enrichment Model (SEM), which can be used to promote challenging and high-end learning in schools. The SEM model accommodates the needs of the gifted student and offers suggestions on how to adjust the level, depth, and enrichment opportunities provided by a curriculum.

Connected Mathematics offers students rich experiences with a variety of mathematical content. Students are introduced to important areas of mathematics, such as combinatorics, graph theory, probability, statistics, and transformational and Euclidean Geometry early in their career so that they can see the vast terrain of mathematics. The algebra strand in *Connected Mathematics* is organized around functions, which are the cornerstone of calculus, and the structure of the real numbers, which brings coherence to the exploration of algebraic ideas.

There are particular features of *Connected Mathematics* which support the mathematically gifted child. In the Teacher's Guides, there are questions in the Launch–Explore–Summarize sequence labeled Going Further that teachers can ask students who are ready to go further mathematically. In the homework ACE assignments, Extensions questions often go beyond what was done in class. Extension questions can be used as additional exercises to push students' thinking. These features, in conjunction with the rich, deep problems offered in this curriculum, provide mathematically gifted students challenging problems to explore each day in class.

Bibliography

The articles, units, and books in this section influenced or supported the development of the CMP philosophy of teaching and learning mathematics.

NCTM (2000). *Principles and Standards for School Mathematics.* Reston, VA.

Phillips, E., G. Lappan, and Y. Grant. (2000). *Implementing Standards-Based Mathematics:* Preparing the Community, the District, and Teachers www.showmecenter.missouri.edu or www.math.msu.edu/cmp

Adams, L. M., K. K. Tung, V. M. Warfield, K. Knaub, B. Mudavanhu, and D. Yong. (2002). Middle School Mathematics Comparisons for Singapore Mathematics, Connected Mathematics Program, and Mathematics in Context. Report submitted to the National Science Foundation by the Department of Applied Mathematics, University of Washington.

American Association for the Advancement of Science: Project 2061. (1999). Middle grades mathematics textbooks: A benchmarks-based evaluation: Evaluation report prepared by the American Association for the Advancement of Science. Washington, D.C.

Anderson, J. R., J. G. Greeno, L. M. Reder, and H. A. Simon. (2000). "Perspectives on Learning, Thinking, and Activity." *Educational Researcher* 29(4):11–13.

Battista, M. T. (February 1999)."The Mathematical Miseducation of America's Youth: Ignoring Research and Scientific Study in Education." *Phi Delta Kappan* 80(6):424–433.

Bay, J. M., B. J. Reys, and R. E. Reys. (March 1999). "The Top 10 Elements that Must Be in Place to Implement Standards-Based Mathematics Curricula." *Phi Delta Kappan* 80(7):503–506.

Ben-Chaim, D., J. Fey, W. Fitzgerald, C. Benedetto, and J. Miller. (1997). A study of proportional reasoning among seventh and eighth grade students. Paper presented at the annual meeting of the American Educational Research Association, Chicago.

Ben-Chaim, D., J. Fey, W. Fitzgerald, C. Benedetto, and J. Miller. (1998). Proportional reasoning among seventh grade students with different curricula experiences. *Educational Studies in Mathematics,* 36:247–73. Kluwer Academic Publishers. The Netherlands.

Ben-Chaim, D., G. Lappan, and R. T. Houang. (1988). "Spatial Visualization: An Intervention Study." *American Educational Research Journal* 25(1):51–57

—"Adolescent's ability to communicate spatial information: Analyzing and effecting students' performance." *Educational Studies in Mathematics* 20:121–146 (1989).

—"The role of visualization in the middle school mathematics curriculum." In T. Eisenberg & T. Drefus, eds., *FOCUS: On Learning Problems in Mathematics* 11(1&2) (1989).

Bouck, M., T. Keusch, and W. Fitzgerald. (1996). Developing as a teacher of mathematics. *The Mathematics Teacher* 89(9): 769–73.

Bruner, J.S. (1960) *The Process of Education.* Cambridge, MA: Harvard University Press.

Carger, C. L. (1997). Attending to new voices. *Educational Leadership* (April), 45–49.

Carrasquillo, A. L., & Rodriguiz, V. (2002). "Language minority students in the mainstream classroom" (2nd ed.). Tonawanda, NY: Multilingual Matters, Ltd.

Corwin, R. B., and S. N. Friel. (1990). *Used Numbers-Statistics: Prediction and Sampling.* White Plains, N. Y.: Dale Seymour Publications.

Dong, Y. R. (2005). "Getting at the content." *Educational Leadership,* 62(4), 14–19.

Fey, J. (May 21–23, 1999)."Standards Under Fire: Issues and Options in the Math Wars." *Summary of Keynote Session at the Show-Me Project Curriculum Showcase.*

Fey, J., and M. K. Heid with R. A. Good, C. Sheets, G. Blume, and R. M. Zbiek. (1995). *Concepts in Algebra: A Technological Approach.* Chicago: Janson Publications, Inc.,

Fey, J., and E. Phillips. (2005) A Course Called Algebra, *Developing Students' Algebraic Reasoning Abilities.* NCSM-Houghton Mifflin Company, School division and McDougal Littell Monograph Series for Leaders in Mathematics Education. Carol Greenes & Carol Findell, Editors. Vol. 3.

Ferrini-Mundy, J., G. Lappan, and E. Phillips. (1996). "Experiences With Algebraic Thinking in the Elementary Grades." *Teaching Children Mathematics.* Reston, Va.: National Council of Teacher of Mathematics.

Fitzgerald, W. and J. Shroyer. (1979). "A Study of the Learning and Teaching of Growth Relationships in the Sixth Grade." *Final Report* NSF SED 77-18545

Friel, S. N. (1998). Teaching Statistics: What's average? In *The Teaching and Learning of Algorithms in School Mathematics:* 1998 Yearbook. Reston, Virginia: National Council of Teachers of Mathematics.

Friel, S. N., J. R. Mokros, and S. J. Russel. (1992). *Used Numbers-Statistics: Middles, Means, and In-Betweens.* White Plains, N.Y.: Dale Seymour Publications.

Friel, S. N. and W. T. O'Connor. (1999). "Sticks to the roof of your mouth?" *Mathematics Teaching in the Middle School,* 4(6):404-11.

Griffin, L. A. Evans, T. Timms, J. Trowell. (2000). Arkansas Grade 8 Benchmarks Exam: How do *Connected Mathematics* schools compare to state data?

Grunow. J. E. (1998). Using concept maps in a professional development program to assess and enhance teachers' understanding of rational number. Doctoral dissertation, University of Wisconsin, Madison.

Herbel-Eisenmann, B. S. (2002). Using student contributions and multiple representations to develop mathematical language. *Mathematics Teaching in the Middle School,* 8(2):100–105.

Herbel-Eisenmann, B., J. P. Smith, J. Star. (1999). Middle school students' algebra learning: Understanding linear relationships in context. Paper presented at the annual meeting of AERA, Montreal.

Hoover, M. N., J. S. Zawojewski, and J. Ridgeway. (1997). Effects of the Connected Mathematics Project on student attainment. Paper presented at the annual meeting of the American Educational Research Association, Chicago.

House, P.A. (Ed.) (1987) Providing opportunities for the mathematically gifted K–12. Virginia: The National Council of Teachers of Mathematics.

Jackson, F. R. (1993). "Seven strategies to support a culturally responsive pedagogy." *Journal of Reading,* 37(4), 52–57.

Jameson, J. H. (1998). Simplifying the language of authentic materials. *TESOL Matters,* p.13.

Keiser, J. M. (1997a). The role of definition in the mathematics classroom. Paper presented at the annual meeting of the American Educational Research Association, Chicago.

Keiser, J. M. (1997b). The development of students' understanding of angle in a non-directive learning environment. Doctoral dissertation, Indiana University, Bloomington.

Keiser, J. M. (2002). "The role of definition." *Mathematics Teaching in the Middle School,* 5(8):506–11.

Kladder, R., J. Peitz, and J. Faulkner. (1998). On the right track. *Middle Ground,* 1(4):32–4.

Kohn, A. (April 1998). "Only for My Kid. How Privileged Parents Undermine School Reform." *Phi Delta Kappan* 79(8):569–577.

Krebs, A. K. (1999). Students' algebraic understanding: A student of middle grades students' ability to symbolically generalize functions. Doctoral dissertation, Michigan State University, East Lansing.

Lambdin, D. and J. M. Keiser. (1996). "The clock is ticking: Time constraint issues in mathematics teaching reform." *Journal of Educational Research,* 90(4):23–32.

Lambdin, D. and G. Lappan. (1997). Dilemmas and issues in curriculum reform: Reflections fron the Connected Mathematics Project. Paper presented at the annual meeting of American Education Research Association, Chicago.

Lambdin, D. V., K. Lynch, and H. McDaniel. (2000). Algebra in the middle grades. *Mathematics Teaching in the Middle School,* 6(3):195–198.

Lambdin, D. and R. Preston. (1995). Caricatures in innovation: Teacher adaptation to an investigation-oriented middle school mathematics curriculum. *Journal of Teacher Education,* 46(2):130–40.

Lapan, R. T., B. J. Reys, D. E. Barnes, and R. E. Reys. (1998). Standards-based middle grade mathematics curricula: Impact on student achievement. Paper presented at the annual meeting of AERA, San Diego.

Lappan, G. (1997). The challenge of implementation: Supporting teachers. *American Journal of Education,* 106(1):207–39.

Lappan, G. and M. K. Bouck. (1998). Developing algorithms for adding and subtracting fractions. In *The Teaching and Learning of Algorithms in School Mathematics: 1998 Yearbook.* Reston, Virginia: National Council of Teachers of Mathematics.

Lappan, G. and R. Even. (1988). "Similarity in the Middle Grades." *Arithmetic Teacher* 35(9):32–35

Lappan, G. and J. Ferrini-Mundy. (1993). "Knowing and Doing Mathematics: A New Vision for Middle Grades Students." *The Elementary School Journal* 93(5):625–641

Lappan, G., and A. F. Friedlander. (1987). "Similarity: Investigations at the Middle Grades Level." In M. Lindquist (Ed.), *Learning and Teaching Geometry,* K-12 NCTM *Yearbook,* 136–140. Reston, Va.: National Council of Teachers of Mathematics.

Lappan, G. and E. Phillips. (1998). Teaching and learning in the Connected Mathematics Project. In *Mathematics in the Middle,* edited by L. Leutzinger. Reston, Virginia: National Council of Teachers of Mathematics.

Lappan, G., and P. Schram. (1989). "Making Sense of Mathematics: Communication and resoning." In P. R. Trafton & A. P. Schulte, eds., *New Directions for Elementary School Mathematics–1989 Yearbook,* 14–30. Reston, Va.: National Council of Teachers of Mathematics.

Lappan, G. and M. J. Winter. (1982). "Spatial Visualization. Mathematics for the Middle Grades (5–9)." NCTM *Yearbook,* L. Silvey and J. Smart, eds., 118–129. Reston, Va.: National Council of Teachers of Mathematics.

Lappan, G., W. Fitzgerald, E. Phillips, M. J. Winter, P. Lanier, A. Madsen-Nason, R. Even, B. Lee, and D. Weinberg. (1998). *The Middle Grades Mathematics Project: The Challenge: Good Mathematics Taught Well.* Final report to the National Science Foundation for Grant No. MDR8318218. East Lansing: Michigan State University.

Lappan, G., E. Phillips, and M. J. Winter. (1984). "Spatial Visualization." *Mathematics Teacher* 77(8):618–623

Lappan, G., E. Phillips, M. J. Winter, and W. Fitzgerald. (1987). "Area Models and Expected Value." *Mathematics Teacher* 80(8):650–658

—"Area Models for Probability." (1993). In *Activities for Active Learning and Teaching,* C. R. Hirsch and R. A. Laing, eds., Reston, Va.: National Council for Teachers of Mathematics.

Linchevski, L. and B. Kutscher. "Tell Me With Whom You're Learning, and I'll Tell You How Much You've Learned: Mixed-Ability vs. Same Ability Grouping in Mathematics." *Journal for Research in Mathematics Education* 29 (5):533–554.

Lipsitz, J., A. W. Jackson, and L. M. Austin. (1997). "What Works in Middle Grades School Reform." *Phi Delta Kappan* March 78 (7):517–556.

Maker, C. J., and A. G. Nielson. (1996). Curriculum development and teaching strategies for gifted learners. (2nd ed.) Austin, TX: Pro-Ed.Edition.

Mathematics and Science Expert Panel for the U. S. Department of Education. (1999). Mathematics and science expert panel: Promising and exemplary mathematics programs, evaluation report prepared for the U.S. Department of Education. Washington, D.C.: U.S. Department of Education.

Miller, J. L., and J. T Fey . (2000). Proportional Reasoning. *Mathematics Teaching in the Middle School,* 5(5): 310–313.

Mullins, I. V. S., M. O. Martin, E. J. Gonzalez, K. M. O'Connor, S. J. Chrostowski, K. D. Gregory, R. A. Garden, T. A. Smith. (2001). *Mathematics Benchmarking Report: TIMSS 1999-Eighth Grade.* Chestnut Hill, Mass.: International Study Center, Lynch School of Education, Boston College.

National Council of Teachers of Mathematics, (2000). *Principles and standards for school mathematics.* Reston, Virginia: National Council of Teachers of Mathematics.

National Council of Teachers of Mathematics. (1989). *Curriculum and Evaluation Standards for School Mathematics.* Reston, Va.: The National Council of Teachers of Mathematics.

National Council of Teachers of Mathematics. (1991). *Professional Standards for Teaching Mathematics.* Reston, Va.: The National Council of Teachers of Mathematics.

National Council of Teachers of Mathematics. (1995). *Assessment Standards for School Mathematics.* Reston, Va.: The National Council of Teachers of Mathematics.

O'Brien, Thomas C. (February 1999). "Parrot Math." *Phi Delta Kappan* 80(6):434–438.

Oguntebi, Z. K. (1983). "Probability: Sex and Grade Level Differences and the Effect of Instruction on the Performance and Attitudes of Middle School Boys and Girls." Ph.D. diss., Michigan State University, East Lansing, Michigan.

O'Neal, S. W. and C. Robinson-Singer. (1998). The Arkansas Statewide Systemic Initiative Pilot of the Connected Mathematics Project: An evaluation report. Report submitted to the National Science Foundation as part of the Connecting Teaching, Learning, and Assessment Project.

Phillips, E. (1991). *Patterns and Functions.* Reston, Va.: The National Council of Teachers of Mathematics.

Phillips, E. and G. Lappan. (1998). "Algebra: The first gate." In *Mathematics in the Middle,* edited by L. Leutzinger. Reston, Virginia: National Council of Teachers of Mathematics.

Peregoy, S. F., and O. F. Boyle. (1997). *Reading, writing, & learning in ESL: A resource book for K-12 teachers.* New York: Longman.

Preston, R. V. and D. V. Lambdin. (1997). Teachers changing in changing times: using stages of concern to understand changes resulting from use of an innovative mathematics curriculum. Paper presented at the annual meeting of the American Educational Research Association, Chicago.

Reinhart, S. C. (2000). "Never say anything a kid can say!" *Mathematics Teaching in the Middle School,* 5(8):478–83.

Renzulli, J. S., and S. M. Reis. (2003). The schoolwide enrichment model: Developing Creative and Productive Giftedness. In N. Colangelo & G. A. Davis (Eds.), *Handbook of Gifted Education* (3rd ed., pp. 184–203). Boston: Allyn & Bacon.

Reys, B., E. Robinson, S. Sconners, and J. Mark. (February 1999). "Mathematics Curricula Based on Rigorous National Standards: What, Why, and How?" *Phi Delta Kappan* 80(6):454-456.

Reys, R. E., B. J. Reys, R. Lapan, G. Holliday, and D. Wasman. (2003). Assessing the impact of standards-based middle school mathematics curriculum materials on student achievement. *Journal for Research in Mathematics Education,* 34(1).

Richard-Amato, P. A., and M. A. Snow. (2005). *Academic success for English language learners: Strategies for K-12 mainstream teachers.* White Plains: Pearson Education.

Rickard, A. (1998). Conceptual and procedural understanding in middle school mathematics. In *Mathematics in the Middle,* edited by L. Leutzinger. Reston, Virginia: National Council of Teachers of Mathematics.

Rickard, A. (1996). Connections and confusion: Teaching perimeter and area with a problem-solving oriented unit. *Journal of Mathematical Behavior,* 15(3):303-27.

Rickard, A. (1995a). Problem solving and computation in school mathematics: Tensions between reforms and practice. *National Forum of Applied Educational Research Journal,* 8(2):41–51.

Rickard, A. (1995b). Teaching with problem-oriented curricula: A case study of middle school mathematics instruction. *Journal of Experimental Education,* 64(1):5–26.

Ridgway, J., J. S. Zawojewski, M. V. Hoover, and D. V. Lambdin. (2003). Student attainment in the Connected Mathematics curriculum. In *Standards-Based School Mathematics Curricula: What Are They? What Do Students Learn?,* edited by S. Senk and D. R. Thompson. Hillsdale, New Jersey: Erlbaum.

Riordan, J. and P. Noyce. (2001). The impact of two standards-based mathematics curricula on student achievement in Massachusetts. *Journal for Research in Mathematics Education,* 32(4):368–398.

Rubenstein, R. N., G. Lappan, E. Phillips, and W. Fitzgerald. (1993). Angle sense: A valuable connection. *Arithmetic Teacher,* 40(6):352–58.

Schoen, H. L., J. T. Fey, C. R. Hirsch, and A. F. Coxford. (February 1999). "Issues and Options in the Math Wars." *Phi Delta Kappan* 80(6):444–453.

Schoenfeld, A., H. Burkhardt, P. Daro, J. Ridgeway, J. Schwartz, and S. Wilcox. (1999). *Balanced Assessment: Middle Grades Assessment.* White Plains, New York: Dale Seymour Publications.

Secada, W. G. (1997). "Understanding in Mathematics & Science." *Principled Practice in Mathematics & Science Education* 1(1):8–9.

Silver, E. A. (1998). "Improving Mathematics in Middle School: Lessons from TIMSS and Related Research." *American Educational Research Journal* 25(1):51–57

Smith, J. P., B. Herbel Eisenmann, and J. Star. (1999). Middle school students' algebra learning: Understanding linear relationships in context. *Proceedings of the 1999 Research Pre-Session of the Annual Meeting of the National Council of Teachers of Mathematics* (NCTM). Reston, Virginia: National Council of Teachers of Mathematics.

Smith, J. P., B. Herbel-Eisenmann, J. Star, A. Jansen. (2000). Quantitative pathways to understanding and using algebra: Possibilities, transitions, and disconnects. Paper presented at the Research Pre-Session of the NCTM annual meeting, Chicago.

Smith, J. P., J. Star, and B. Herbel-Eisenmann. (2000). Studying mathematical transitions: How do students navigate fundamental changes in curriculum and pedagogy? Paper presented at the 2000 annual meeting of AERA, New Orleans.

Smith, J. P., E. A. Phillips, and B. Herbel-Eisenmann. (October 1998). Middle school students' algebraic reasoning: New skills and understandings from a reform curriculum. *Proceedings of the 20th Annual Meeting of the PME, North American Chapter,* 173–78, Raleigh.

Smith, J. P. and E. A. Phillips. (2000). "Listening to Middle School Students' Algebraic Thinking." *Mathematics Teaching in the Middle School,* 6(3):156–161.

Star, J., B. A. Herbel-Eisenman, and J. P. Smith III. (2000). "Algebraic Concepts: What's Really New in New Curricula?" *Mathematics Teaching in the Middle School,* 5(7):446-451

Van Zoest, L. R., and A. Enyart. (1998). "Discourse, of Course: Encouraging Genuine Mathematical Conversations." *Mathematics Teaching in the Middle School,* 4(3):150–157

Winking, D., A. Bartel, and B. Ford. (1998). The Connected Mathematics Project: Helping Minneapolis middle school students 'beat the odds': Year one evaluation report. Report submitted to the National Science Foundation as part of the Connecting Teaching, Learning, and Assessment Project.

Zawojewski, J. S., M. Robinson, M. V. Hoover. (1999). Reflections on mathematics and the Connected Mathematics Project. *Mathematics Teaching in the Middle School,* 4(2):324–30.

Zwiers, J. (2005). "The third language of academic English." *Educational Leadership,* 62(4), 60–63.